Twice I Refused to Stay Dead

Near Death Experience

HOW TO USE MEDITATION – VISUALIZATION - and SELF-HYPNOSIS KEEP YOURSELF HEALTH

Copyright.Gov © 2025
1-14876938113

Jeri Lee C.Ht.

Twice
I Refused to Stay Dead

Near Death Experience

HOW TO USE MEDITATION – VISUALIZATION and SELF-HYPNOSIS KEEP YOURSELF HEALTH

ISBN: 978-0-692-68476-4

DEDICATION

IN MEMORY OF KATHLEEN INEZ LEE
SEPT 25 1937   SEPT 28 1991

An epitaph to "MY THEE"
Great Lady Kathy Lee
Thank you for being you
And letting me be me.
You gave so much then,
Took the same to give
And give again
You have been missed so very much
By every soul you touched.
Cradled deep within our hearts
You planted the seed of love.
We nourished it with loving tears
In the caves of our loneliness.
Now, it has blossomed for all to see
The reflection of your image.
I know you found that perfect peace
In the light at the end of the trail,
Total nothingness.
Now pause, then rest,
And begin once again your cycle
Of happiness.

"YOUR THEE"

KATHY LEE

Twice I Refused to Stay Dead

Jeri Lee C.Ht.

TABLE OF CONTENTS

DEDICATION... v
INTRODUCTION.. x

CHAPTER   1 Phase one Healing technique.......... 1
CHAPTER   2 Phase one Healing technique........ 15
CHAPTER   3 Phase one Healing technique...... 32
CHAPTER   4 Condensed Version.................. 46
CHAPTER   5 Overview............................ 61
CHAPTER   6 Self Hypnosis........................ 65
CHAPTER   7. Hypnosis............................ 77
CHAPTER   8. Meditation........................... 93
CHAPTER   9. Pineal Gland...................... 109
CHAPTER 10. Visualization......................123
CHAPTER 11. Memory............................ 134
CHAPTER 12. Theory of Mind................... 140
CHAPTER 13. Consciousness..................... 150
CHAPTER 14. Sounds and Vibrations........... 170
CHAPTER 15. Singing to Yourself............... 181
CHAPTER 16. The Brain.......................... 191
CHAPTER 17. Thought and Color................ 202
CHAPTER 18. Using your Senses................. 230
CHAPTER   Conclusion......................... 240

INTRODUCTION

Let us analyze the most important single word in our vocabulary, "LIFE." Without it nothing would exist, as it is the universal condition of all existence. It is physical in form but Quantum in reality.

Wikipedia states that, "life is a characteristic distinguishing physical entity having biological processes from those that do not, either because such functions have ceased because of death or because they lack such functions and are classified as inanimate."

Encyclopedia Britannica says, "Although life is a noun, 8juuuuuuuas with other defined entities, the word life might be better cast as a verb to reflect its essential status as a process."

The Cambridge Dictionary shortens it as, "Life is the period between birth and death, or the state of being alive."

Life and living should be our natural concern and the unconscious goal of our body, mind, and soul. Primary in this journey is the quality and length of that space called Life. My intentions for this book are to create an understanding of the difference between living and existing. Then show you how you can control that outcome by a few simple exercises. Life is simple, living it is complicated, and controlling it is a lifetime challenge.

This challenge is the motivation that promotes your lifestyle, ambitions, and accomplishments. However, like most things in your environment you probably take life and living for granted and won't appreciate it either until you're about to lose them. Then out of fright and panic, you apply Band-Aids or a fix it fast fad, to this body you have spent a lifetime abusing.

The search is on and as part of this mid-life panic you expend your energy and monetary savings to find that elusive fountain of youth. In despair you realize it is a mirage sought after by many and found by few.

In this book, I intend to show you that the fountain of youth is inside, it is your magic mirror. Face yourself and stare into your own eyes until you can see yourself, really see yourself. The eyes are said to be the windows to your soul so open your windows and find your soul, because that is where it all happens.

You were given the gift of life and living came along for the ride, from that point nothing is free. If you want to find yourself, along with that fountain of youth, you must work for it. When you just follow the crowd, doing what seems enjoyable, going with the flow, you are not living, but are only existing. There is a great difference when you take control of your life and design it to benefit your greatest potential.

There is only one tool that can accomplish this, it is creative thought and thinking. You might say you are always thinking, but I will argue that routine thoughts are mundane habits you learn by rote, memorize by repetition and recite daily as your pattern of life. Creative thoughts are formed when you take a look at the inside of your dreams and stop following the footprints made by others. The production of an original thought form is one that belongs to you. It is not something you heard or co-authored it is something you created. It is the first step in taking control of who and what you have the potential of being.

In the silent moments of our deepest thoughts live commonly unspoken questions. Everyone thinks about it and is unwilling to ask. When will I die and how will it happen? Since this book is designed to help you with that concern, I consider it a proper question to address. If you knew the time and date of your death would that make living your life any different? Would you work harder at keeping your body healthy if you knew you were living in it until age 90 or more? Would you lose hope and stop fighting for life if you knew you were not going to win? Life is worth living and death is an unknown, I have done both but as of now I am on the side of life and doing my best to stay there.

My hope is that you can learn something from this book about yourself and how to keep your body healthy by seeing how I have managed to keep myself going for many years. I am not applauding myself for some great accomplishment, and I realize I am not the only one that shares similar experiences. It gives authority and authenticity to these pages because I walked the walk and did not imagine these stories. My basic hope is that I can put quantum ideas into an understandable format, showing that life is magical and that you are your personal puppeteer.

Quantum is a metaphysical term that gives us a license to form theories on and about the things in our reality that we know exist but cannot scientifically prove. Such theories as: the mind, soul, spirit, thought, consciousness, and many others. I can explain my theories about the way I perceive these units of subatomic matter, but I cannot show you, their photos. Of course, neither can our most prestigious physicists. It all interplays with life and death because life is the number one Quantum question mark. What is it, where did it come from and where did it go?

With all that, it's time to take a walk, and I might be morbid, but I like to walk through graveyards. Especially, when I can find an old one, the older, and the better. I read the engravings on the stones that mark the memory of someone's life. They usually have the name and year of birth and death. But between these two dates there is a dash, which is the most interesting part because that is the life between two points in time. That is where you insert the story of each of these lives. Every cemetery is a library of suspense stories with lost secrets and words that were never spoken. If each DASH came to life for one last day what song would it sing?

As a child, my grandmother escorted me through the old family plot on the homestead in. She introduced me to my ancestors and often told special little stories that went along with the introduction. Like, this is your great grandma; she died in childbirth when your grandpa was born. Your great-grandfather then married her sister.

In another cemetery, she cried over the stones on two small graves and told the stories of the two babies that did not live. As an adult, I was able to understand myself better through these stories. Today I can visit the graves of my parents, and both sets of grandparents and get them all into one photo. How is that for a family portrait?

Learn something about yourself by taking a walk through your local cemetery as if it were the local park. Take the time to listen to the voices that hover around the stones, and to talk to them. Your first response is probably fear, and I ask, of what? You are the only one there, or are you? I have found as I cross the country if I must sleep in my vehicle the safest place is in the graveyard, and I have done it often.

The most interesting stones have a legacy in the form of an epitaph, such as loving husband, caring mother. Here are several notable ones:

"The sole purpose of life is to gain merit for life in

eternity." St Augustine [354-430]

""Those who in living fill the smallest space, in death have often left the greatest void." W.S. Landor [1775-1864]

"Count your nights by stars, not shadows; count your life with smiles, not tears." [Italian Proverb]

"Of all the sad words of tongue or pen the saddest are these: "It might have been" John Greenleaf Whittier [1807-1892]

"The soul would have no rainbow, had the eyes no tears." John Vance Cheney [1848-1922]

"Comforts in Heaven, and we are on earth, where nothing lives but crosses, cares and grief." William Shakespeare [1564-1616]

"Here lies my husband Joe, all dressed up and no place to go."

Ask yourself what few words your grandkids would read on that dash between the dates on your stone. Hopefully mine will say, "I took the time to live." The first date on my stone is 1939-???? In this book, I will explain how you can stretch the dash between your dates. My second date has already been stamped twice -1985 and then -2005. But somehow it has not been set in stone yet, as it is 2015, and I just had my 76th birthday.

I am sure that everyone has reached a plateau in life where

they look back and ask themselves many questions about the trail, they left from birth to now. It has been poetically entitled a walk down memory lane. That is an extremely popular address because most people on the planet have their personal address at memory lane. Everything about you, me or us is personal, and it is your personal identity reflected in your history that makes you the person you are today. That is what this book is all about.

Yes, you made yourself the person you are today and are continuing to fashion yourself into the person you will be tomorrow. This might not be something you agree with but stop and think about all the decisions you had to make to become todays you. It just did not happen with one wave of a magical wand, and it might not have ended up being what you wanted. You have the ability to accomplish your dreams and become that person you want to be. It is never too late to accomplish your potential.

On my 70th birthday, I wrote this poem to myself and then ran away from home. But that's another story, the story in this book is how I managed to live long enough to write it. If I die before I am 90 or 100 it does not mean that my technique did not work because I have already kept myself going for 30 years, living the book I am writing. But I will share my poem.

Jeri Lee C.Ht.

Reflection

Hello Mirror on my wall.
I have no secrets you tell all.
Behind this wrinkled face of age
A child of memories plays on my stage.
The riddle of time has etched life's change.
While deep inside I remain the same.
For others, I wear the mask of fate.
I took time to live that's how I rate.
The ups and downs the good and bad.
Life's challenges were often sad.
Though my body grew old
My mind stayed young.
My spirit is actively searching for fun.
So old lady just step aside
And let my memories take a ride.

There are some things in life that are possible and some that are not. It is impossible to think two thoughts at the same time, and it is impossible to take two steps at one time. With this in mind, it is possible to have a single thought and jump into your wish. It is possible to think of anything you want yourself while bearing in mind that the laws of nature are the guiding force. It is possible that by visualizing yourself healthy you can reach that goal one step at a time.

Your mind has your DNA blueprint from which to manifest your wishes, and although the mind can change DNA, your mind must support a form of logic. It can repair an injured limb but is not capable of manufacturing one if you were born without it.

The unfair thing about life is its destination, and the fact that the day you reach the end of that road is the day you are most qualified to live that life. Life is tough, and it took a lot of learning to get to that last day, only to find that your reward for all that hard work is death.

I have made it my challenge in life to outlive death or to give it a run for my life. So, I have created my song of life, and you can learn to sing it also, so let's go for a ride.

In the late 60's, while attending an Airstream Rally in Laramie Wyoming I met the entrepreneur of Colonel Sanders Chicken, Mr. Harlan Sanders himself. Born in 1890 he was at that time in his late 70's and an active keynote speaker. At that time, I had just turned 30 and in my way of thinking he was an old man. He was extremely interesting, and I was impressed that he started the chicken business at age 65 after he retired from a military career. It has taken me an additional 45 years to up and realize the reality of the wisdom he inspired in others and me. He dared to be creative in his thinking and chase his dreams. Grandma Mosses [Anna Mary Robertson Moses] is another who in 1936 [three years before I was born] started her famous career as an artist at age 76 [my age now]. So may I share her success and fortune at the same age? I must add that Grandma Moses lived to be 101, which is my goal. My great aunt was 102 and my great three times grandfather was 107, and I will bet that all these special persons sang their special songs.

Life is unfair because energy is being wasted on the young, it should be shared with the old, who would appreciate it and not take it for granted. Living is rough, and it takes a lot of our time just to get old, we spend most of that time learning and once we are full of knowledge we die taking it all with us. So why do we work so hard to become intelligent and wise, when the day after our funeral we will not be missed? Just think if energy was balanced out across your lifetime. You would not have made so many stupid mistakes in your youth or need the nursing home when you got old. You could just keep on working and would not need SSI. Then because you knew ahead the time and place of your death you just took your glass of Champaign and posed for your death photo. Or was that a 'Mint Julep'?

What is Life?

The whispers of the restless winds
The babble of the brook
The chirping of the wild birds
The heartbeat of a loved one
The sounds of a tender voice
The touch that sooths all heartache
A smile that gives you bliss
The wisdom of the ages
The truth we all behold.
The echo of forever
Our memories seamed in gold
Knock on that door of ages.
Enter your dreams and see
Share those dreams with others.
For life is not, unless you are living
So listen to the silent one
The self that dwells within
For it will show you right from wrong
And teach you how to live.

There are thousands of theories on what life is, but only one fact. LIFE is a reality and it is up to you to live

CHAPTER ONE

Phase One Healing Technique

While going through airline security several weeks ago, the attendant said you must take off your shoes unless you are 75. "I am," was my response. She gave me that, are you for real, look, as I flashed my ID and kept on walking. Last month I visited Wal-Mart hair salon where every visit is a new experience. In the course of generating casual conversation, I asked the beautician what color she would call my hair. Her answer was, "I would say it's brown tinted with blonde speckled with a few grays." I then asked, "Well is that a typical color for 75-year-old? "Not sure," was her reply, " but no way are you 75." Not wanting to insult her judgment I said, " Yeah, well I'm 65 +10." This answer seemed suitable the next day when I went to an all-you-can-eat buffet; they informed me that, you must be 65 to qualify for the senior menu. Then only yesterday I answered the phone and ended up talking to a salesperson asking for donations for some organization. To which I responded I "I am 75, and you should be giving me things not trying to take them from me." Her comeback was, "Well you sure don't sound like an old lady."

I'm not sure how a 75-year-old lady is supposed to look or sound. But my point here is, I found a way to look and sound younger than whatever fits that description. Even though I have had two near-death experiences and lived with a pacemaker since 1985. I have survived lead extraction with emergency open-heart surgery, leaving me with serious heart problems. I have survived cancer and lived with lupus for 30 years while being labeled a type 2 diabetic. I had blood disorder that was just shy of a total bleed out. Probably if I listened to what all the doctors told me I could list many more. Since doctors did not have the answers, I needed to stay healthy; I was compelled to invent a cure or rehabilitation program for my disorders.

Knowing that "Necessity was the Mother of invention," I started a program for myself including meditation, visualization, and self-hypnosis. I refer to it as Phase One, from 1985 to 1991. I improved my techniques for Phase Two, from 1992 to 2005 then again from 2005 to date I have been updating, collaborating and perfecting the original program, and I label that Phase Three.

While reading this book, have no doubt, that my program works even though it may seem at times that the 'fate of death' has had its hand around my neck. I assure you; I don't slow down long enough for it to catch me. To date, I have kept myself alive for 30 years using my program. I plan to be around for another 20 years BUT don't think that the program did not work if I die before age 90 to 100. You can do the same by just following a few simple suggestions. There are no gimmicks, nothing to buy, no special pills to take. You were born with all the necessary equipment to keep yourself young and healthy, all you need is the instruction manual on how to use the abilities you have possessed your entire life. You now hold in your hands that manual that will instruct you on how to use your voice, mind power, and determination to visualize yourself healthy, wealthy, and wise. Although our environment influences us, this is a process that you must do for yourself. Remember that you alone are in charge of producing personal success or failure because what you are today is the exact outcome of what you produced based on all the decisions you have made over your lifetime.

The first three chapters of this book are a detailed rendition of my life with the how's and when's. I hang no labels on myself; I put no fences around my mind, and I judge no one for what they think or what I think they are thinking. I surround myself with white light while juggling rainbows and listen to the messages in my head that I eagerly investigate while trying to keep my body as young as my mind thinks it is.

My two sons ages 52 & 53 along with other parts of my immediate family keep saying to me "why don't you act your age?" My answer is, "I would rather act the age I want to be," and usually do. Case in point: The flight I took a couple weeks ago to LAX, Los Angeles California, was

 to attend my graduation from college. On September 19, 2014; dressed in a blue cap and gown with the traditional Golden Tassel I proudly marched to the music in my head singing, "Memories are made of this." I joined the graduating class of HMI held at the picturesque Calamigos Ranch in Malibu. We were the 46th class to graduate from Hypnosis Motivation Institute of Hypnotherapy in Tarzana Ca. HMI has earned the distinction of being the first nationally accredited hypnotherapy college in the US.

On Feb 3, 2013, I completed the QHHT [Quantum Healing Hypnosis Therapy] classes taught by the late Dolores Cannon. I received her highest-level certification as a Dedicated Practitioner specializing in past life regression and quantum hypnosis therapy.

At age 75, I decided it was time to get a diploma for the career I started over 65 years ago when as a child I hypnotized my father's chickens and my mother's cats. Being reprimanded for my actions, they explained that chickens laid eggs, and the cats must catch mice. Then they asked the big question: "Where did you get such a strange idea?" So, hypnotherapy and self-hypnosis have lurked in the shadow of my life as I pursued other careers. The first was as a commercial artist and technical illustrator, then as a Renaissance artist producing uniquely unusual jewelry labeled new age or occult. After that, I went to the dogs, breeding and showing rare toy breeds until age 70. It was then I decided to run away from home and for two years I survived totally off the grid. I learned a lot about myself and today I'm now old enough to know better and wise enough to help others. QHHT along with HMI provides the perfect springboard for my fourth and final career as, "Spiritgaea Presents, Hypnotherapist and Author, Jeri Lee C.Ht."

The ideas that I am presenting to you are my original ideas, practiced and modified since 1985 when I tasted death and the need to survive. Over the past 30 years, I have researched and developed this technique and credit to it the fact that I have learned to understand myself and to maintain a quality of life while doing it. Since I am the living testimony of my techniques, I deem it necessary to include parts of my life story. It will show how I created this method and how it had produced successful effects in my life and health. For those who wish to have the condensed version of 'technique only,' skip to chapter 4. For those who crave detail, question reason, and logic, or have a passion for words, please keep reading.

Disclaimer: I'm not a doctor, so I have no rights to prescribe anything in the line of medicine. I cannot tell you to stop taking your collection of pills, but I can suggest that you review them with your doctor. I am a certified hypnotherapist, qualified to increase motivation or alter behavior pattern as a counselor and hypnotherapist. It is with this motive in mind that I write this book.

Southern California, June 12, 1985, was a warm summer day, and my psyche claimed it was a good day to die. The 911 call brought red lights and paramedics to my home to hopefully prevent my departure from this plane of existence. This scene was deja vu from three days before.

Being a street artist, my partner and I traveled, sometimes long distances to do art shows. The past weekend we had a street show in Sunnyvale Ca and since I was not feeling that great instead of returning home, which was an 8-hour trip, we spent the night with a friend. Monday morning, I needed emergency assistance, and an ambulance took me to the nearest hospital. It happened to be Kaiser Permanente. They connected me to an IV and did an EKG then after a couple hours, sent me on my way, even though I could not stand up. They knew I had a serious problem, but I was only a street artist that did not have insurance, so they did not want to admit me. They could probably have prevented the major stroke I had three days later. They sent me to the street to die.

I spent the long trip home in the camper bed not able to sit or exit the camper. Then it all got worse; my heart had decided to play patty cake, patty cake with PVC's [premature ventricular contractions] and fibrillation while its natural pacemaker went on vacation. I was having a stroke. I was not in pain; I was not anything, just an existence that was slowly losing consciousness.

Now, the second call to 911 and I was taken to Victorville hospital. They stabilized me, then decided they could do nothing to help. But since I owned property and paid taxes to San Bernardino County, I was qualified for county assistance, so I was sent by ambulance over the mountain to San Bernardino County hospital. This trip etched itself in my memory as a day that would change my life in more than one way. I recall that I could see the shadows of two attendants leaning over me with tubes, syringes, and needles while in the background the driver's voice was heard requesting emergency instructions to keep me alive.

As the ambulance crested the top of Cajon Pass and started down the mountain, I was on top of existence. My spirit had different ideas and decided it was time to leave the body, I remember floating out of the ambulance, or perhaps through it. I glided gracefully over the clouds that covered San Bernardino Valley in a sense of total peace. It was like I was in the ambulance then I was out. I did not follow a tunnel or visit my deceased relatives as some stories tell. I was aware of a bright light but was in no hurry to get there. I glided over the puffy white clouds that looked like miniature marshmallows floating on a sea of smog. I felt calm and peaceful as I looked back viewing the frustration occurring over my limp body. It didn't seem to bother me; I was just content in this space. It was absolute peace like I belonged here. I floated over the valley watching all the people on the ground. I felt like a bird looking down at the human race. They appeared as a colony of intoxicated ants, millions of beings running to and fro, oblivious to their real purpose for existence. They acted like mundane forms of ectoplasm in search of the roadmap of life. I felt a real sadness for humankind and reached out for the answers to add meaning and direction to human existence.

Instantly the answer was there, all the answers, to everything, in an instant I knew, I knew everything. To think was to be. In an instant, I knew that answers to life are so simple. Humans confuse their existence by making it too complex for them to understand, and then they create superior deities to credit the good and blame the bad. The secret of life is that there are no secrets because nature is an open book. Life is the reward for the living, and every atom has its individual form of life.

I now understood existence, but I was dying, did everyone understand at death? It was then I heard the voice of knowing, and it said, "Mankind complicates the simplicity of his environment by creating imaginary solutions for the things he does not understand."

"How can I help them?" was my thought. And the voice answered, "You can only show them, they must help themselves." I then saw the light, a large globe of ectoplasm with a vortex in its center, and it seemed like I was viewing an inter-dimensional space. It could have been a hologram; it looked like an image from a projector reflecting off the clouds in much the same way as the sun projects a rainbow.

The image was dazzling, so I closed my eyes. The voice said, "Open your eye; the only one that sees the truth, the one inside your head; look and see and know, because the light of the body is the eye." "If, therefore, thine eye be single, thy whole body shall be full of light." [Math.6: 22 the single eye is the spiritual third eye, the pineal gland.]

I opened my eyes, and I looked, I was inside an enormous library with endless rows and volumes of manuscripts. And the voice said, "It's all there, everything you could want or need to know, and you can access it by raising your consciousness to this level. You see it as you think it should appear when in truth there is no library that contains words because the truth has no language, it just is. It is just knowing."

It was then that the cosmic adrenalin kicked in; I could not die. I had a mission; I had to explain to humanity the simplicity of their complex existence. I had to help them see how easy it was to attain immortality and to be at peace with their God-self. I had to explain to them the continuity of consciousness and its universal links to the cosmic design.

I had a big job to do - I could not die and heard myself shout 'I WILL NOT DIE' as I came crashing back into my body. I remember the speed of my re-entry and the impact of my landing that forced me to cry out in pain as I tried to move my body. I could think, but I could not talk. I was back at my own request, and now I had to make the best out of it, so let the challenges begin.

With the help of a pacemaker to keep my heart beating, I slowly recovered from the stroke that nearly killed me at age 45. I knew I had a mission, I knew I had tasted the fruit of the tree of life and held the key to the book of knowledge. I also realized that the book was written in a universal language of concepts, which could not be easily translated into words. The book of knowledge is the book of conscious knowing.

All humankind has an awareness of this knowing that becomes his driving force in the search for the reasons of life. For centuries, we have been crippled by; organized religions, corrupt governments, and greedy businesses. They have locked the doors to spiritual growth, insight, and advancement. Our real history is not what they taught. Our educators have blinded humankind with avenues of darkness. It is time for us to know the truth, see the light and wake up and to become aware. Knowing brings personal responsibility for caring for your environment on all its planes of existence. We are custodians of this planet earth as well as its spiritual worlds, and at this time collectively we have failed greatly on all accounts.

On that day in 1985, they installed my first pacemaker and said to me "We fixed you. Now stand up and walk." Well, that all sounded great, but the reality was I could stand up and take a few steps, then with energy depleted I had to sit or fall. I did not have the strength to function, either in body or mind. If I were to get excited or show any emotion, I would pass out. The medical profession did not want to deal with me. I was without insurance and did not qualify for a welfare program, so even my care at a county hospital with co-pay was limited to only the necessities with no details. So, they released me to the world to live or die, either way without their help. They did give me a bandage, in the form of a prescription labeled "quinidine," with instructions to take it every 6 hours.

As I was too weak to walk, I had to rely on a wheelchair and to be pushed around. I was frustrated because I had all this stuff in my head that I wanted to tell. But every time I opened my mouth to speak, words came out of my mouth that were not part of my thinking. It was as if someone else talked while I was trying to think, but we were not on the same page and often not even in the same book. I later learn that your left and right hemispheres of the brain can function independently of each other after a physical trauma. So patience was a lesson I had to learn. My left-brain thought it was the boss, and it had to learn to shut-up and listen to what the right brain was saying. Once I did this, I started learning things that I never dreamed I knew.

That started in June, and now it is September, and I was still being pushed around in a wheelchair and getting weaker instead of stronger. The doctor still said," there is nothing wrong with you. Stand up and walk," But by now

I was in so much pain I cried when I moved, and my arms lying across my body hurt so badly I could not sleep.

Before this all happened, we had purchased property in Missouri and planned to move to be in the center of the US, giving us easier access to more art shows and Renaissance fairs. So in the middle of my pain, we moved from California to Missouri. That is where I have lived since 1985, in the middle of the Woods, at the end of the road, on 70 acres of wooded land, with two caves and several waterfalls.

Having just read a book by Fred Soyka titled "The ION effect" I realized if anything would bring me back to health this property would. The ion book details how air contains negative and positive ions and that the negative one helps support the oxygen in your body making you feel better. This information showed that the most favorable ion to generate good health is a negative ion. The most convenient location for the abundance of negative ionization is in front of a cave or facing the ocean breeze or a waterfall. Having two caves and several waterfalls as my yard I slowly weaned myself from the wheelchair but had a limited radius of activity while still faithful taking my quinidine pills every six hours.

While visiting a friend, she recommended I see her psychic for answers the doctors could not give me, so I did. My primary interest was for the psychic to tell me what my real problem was and how to correct it. In the course of my reading, the psychic made a statement, "What you have is Lupus, no it is not Lupus but is just like Lupus." Well, that sounded great, but I had no idea what Lupus was and soon forgot what she had told me. I just knew I had to find another doctor. Three months and several doctors later I heard the doctor say to me "What you have is Lupus, no it is not Lupus but is just like Lupus." Well, my ears perked up, and he had my trust. He said, "stop taking the quinidine it is giving you Lupus."

From that point, I started my walk to wellness with my pacemaker as security along with caves waterfalls and negative ionization and a doctor that cared. I had been previously trained in meditation, visualization and self-hypnosis but temporally discounted their power. So, now that I could think again, I started an obedient discipline of taking time each day to find myself and see life with a single eye.

Twice I Refused to Stay Dead

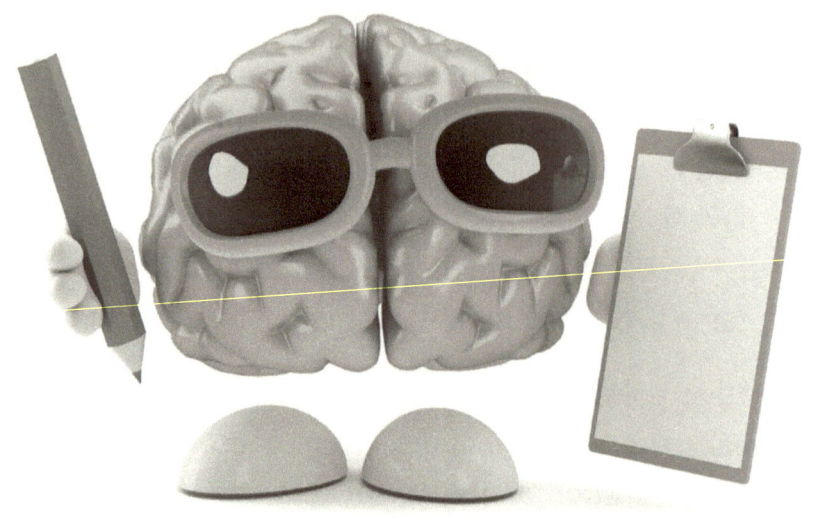

CHAPTER TWO

Phase Two Healing Technique

It was a cool, crisp October morning in 1991 and September had dealt me the worst blow of my entire life, for it had just stolen my reason for living. The dark arm of Death wrapped its cloak, labeled lymphoma, around the love of my life and snatched her without warning, leaving a canyon in my chest where my heart use to be. The trauma of realizing the finality of death was almost unbearable. My entire existence was shattered, without direction and in a state of non-reality. I was expecting the nightmare to end, but it didn't, and I couldn't seem to wake myself.

> "Ragged leaves, Tattered remnants of the storm,
> Lonely transients, In the October morn.
> Feed gently, Restless Browsing breeze,
> On thinning stock, Of trembling leaves.
> Angled branches, Framing azure sky.
> Sharper, clearer, By and by.
> Bones only, Now bare exposed,
> Supplicant To November's snow."

I was now the sole owner of 70 acres of canyons and caves, one of the most beautiful places on God's green earth, with no reason for existing. Why her? Why me? What did I do to deserve this? Old people are supposed to die, and she was only 54. You are supposed to be sick a long time before you die, she lasted only three months. The doctors said the chemo would cure her, and she would be fine by Xmas. Now, how do I put the pieces back together? How do I start over? Where do I begin? I lived in the woods, at the end of the road, all by myself. I have three small dogs and thirteen cats, three horses, four milking goats and a dozen chickens. I hugged the dogs, patted the cats and in total frustration, I took a long walk.

Climbing to the highest point on the walls that framed my valley I stood on the edge of the cliff directly above the wide-open mouth of my largest cave. It is the mouth of mother earth, and if you listen closely, she will talk to you. I was ready to listen. I took three deep breaths, breathing in the freshness of the fall country air and the powerful Ions from the cave beneath me. Off in the distance, I could hear the waterfall as it softly played the symphony of Caves Springs Ranch. The trees around me were taking on the color of an autumn artist's palette. As I watched, they dropped to the canvas floor one by one to produce their masterpiece. The sun was just now entering the gate on the far east corner of my yard about 1/4 mile away, and as it reached me, I smiled with happy thoughts and a broken heart. We had determined that this was a power point because of the large stone that shared our special spot. We often sat on this power stone and watched the sunrise. It was about four feet in diameter with a flat top, so we referred to it as a sacrificial altar.

I sat on the altar facing south. With eyes closed, palms open to the heavens and gently resting on each knee, I put myself into a state of meditation. I was looking for answers to my questions and a reason for living. The four winds blew around me taking me back in my childhood, to that little white Bible my parent's gifted me with at age eight. It was practically worn out by age 16 when they replaced it with a new black one. At that age, I had a photographic memory and rewarded myself with colored stars to indicate the verses or chapters I memorized. Today reveals that the tattered little book is extremely colorful. I just wished I still had that special memory.

The four winds as mentioned in many cultural ceremonies are also referred to, in the Bible; the Hebrew word for "wind" can also mean "spirit." The Native American tradition of the medicine wheel indicates the four winds are also spirits. In my meditation, I was reminded that these four points are everything, everywhere, but likewise part of me. My memories also took me back to 1989 when I had invited a medicine woman from New Mexico to visit my land; her granddaughter, the medicine woman in training, accompanied her. They perform a daylong ceremony, as we walked the land visiting Power spots and ending with the campfire. The medicine-women also blessed the altar I am sitting on while talking to the ancestors that once lived here. With respect to self and all things natural, we dedicated this land to Mother Earth.

We continually find evidence that this valley was once inhabited by a culture that used arrows and stone tools, as we have found many of them. There are places where the earth looks like it burped knapping chips evidence of arrow point production. Out of respect for Mother Nature and the early American culture that once occupied my land I stood and saluted the four winds.

With my arms lifted high above embracing the blue sky, I defiantly declared to my visible world, " you are mine, all that I see I own, this is my world". Then in the silence of my broken heart my world laughed at me, then my trees laughed at me, and even the sky laughed at me as the winds began to blow. I turned to the winds with my ceremonial whistle in hand; It was a wing bone of my totem bird, a gift from a shaman. I blew it four times to give respect to each of the four winds. Then I faced the East where the sun entered my valley each morning, and I gave thanks to the Mother, from whence life began. Then I blew again for I was twice born first of the spirit than as a form. I then blessed the Earth, knowing she greets the Father sun each morning as it embraces her, giving vitality and life to a new day while also enriching my daily life. Through the wind of the East, I ask for wisdom to defeat my ego. And to also soften my pain so I could gain insight into death, logic and reason. As the sun gives me, the light to see may it also give me wisdom? I breathe in the color Yellow from its rays to cleanse myself.

Turning South, I saluted the wind that gave warmth in my new life, that I could overcome loneliness, heal my emotional void, and retrieve my heart. All this: while enriching my life with courage, ambitions and desires to fulfill my destiny. I paused and breathed in the light. The clear White light to vitalize me with the rainbows it carries. Now I blow my whistle to salute the West, that direction that gives me an insight into myself with the ability to love and care for others. While I explore my inherent quest to know my source of creation and to deal with the finality of my existence. Claiming Red as its color, I breathed in vitality, then softened it to pink for love. I was fully aware that this was the station of procreation as well as the creation.

Turning clockwise, I faced the North and blew my whistle in the direction of reincarnation. Here I find the time to reflect on the self, bringing spirituality, understanding and completion to life. Along with the message that my soul shouts to me daily as it echoes in the chambers of my primal memories, as it migrates through my daily activities challenging my dreams, desires and accomplishments. The north is colored black and like a black hole it absorbs everything and will eventually give it all back. Here I paused to collect my emotions.

Raising my whistle high to the heavens, I blew it for my

inner self-giving thanks for the power, strength and love of the spirit world that rides on the winds and whispers to me in my dreams. Once again, I blew my ceremonial whistle then breathed in the winds. I could taste the freshness of life and feel its energy caressing me. I closed my eyes and focused on drawing in the color of that light as a liquid rainbow. I heard the sound of the wind accompanied by its cosmic choir. I tasted the freshness of life in the air as it enhanced my chakras to vitalize my being with that special knowing that her spirit will always live in my Aura. At peace with myself, I took her spirit hand and slowly we once again walked together back to the cabin we called home.

Jeri Lee C.Ht.

Memories

"A thread-thin tie now
To all that was and would not be -
Return like unasked guests.
To an empty table
In a large and vacant house.
The partners dance at arm's length
To the sound of the wind in the trees,
But night will come.
And tears will bathe the forest,
And refresh the thirsty earth.
Tomorrow's hope is built of truth,
If hope exists at all:
So, courage, friend,
And maybe in some distant place
On new-found paths, we'll meet again.
The vacant house has many rooms,
Each waiting to be found."

One month later and seemingly overnight a five-pound sarcoma blossomed in my right thigh, and I was certain the Angels are singing my song. For fourteen years we were inseparable, so perhaps this was my door to the other side. My studies have revealed that it is a common event when you go through a major stress or trauma if there is a weak spot in your body it might erupt without warning.

Of course, I panicked and went to visit a doctor when I first noticed the swelling. She said, "looks like a blood clot to me, get off your feet, keep your legs elevated and take aspirins to thin your blood then come back in a couple weeks." Well, two weeks later it was twice the size and growing.

It was about this point in my story that I started talking to myself along with the spirits that lived with me. I pretended I was talking to the animals that also lived in my house. Oh, by the way, I forgot to mention it also included three parrots.

I am sure at some given time you have heard; only old people talk to themselves, or if you talk to yourself then you must be crazy. Well, my thinking was I am getting older, perhaps I've reached the point where it's okay to talk to myself, or perhaps, I don't care if people think I'm crazy. The only ears to hear me are my animals, and they love me unconditionally, they think I'm talking to them, which makes them happy. Maybe, I told myself if I talk out loud the birds might start talking back to me. So out of necessity and desperation I carried on a lengthy conversation with myself while teaching myself to communicate with my best teachers, me, myself and I.

The next day they performed a CT to my thigh and found that a massive tumor occupied two-thirds of my right thigh. It was impossible to live with, so my doctor referred to a surgeon who introduced himself to me while flirting with his nurse. My preliminary exam included this statement; "there is nothing wrong with your leg except that fat ladies have fat legs." I asked if he had viewed the films I delivered to him and he said, "No, he had not had time." Then he looked at the film and said, "As it says, it looks like a lipoma that is too much fat." "Guess you can't read," was my come back, " it says that it is most likely a liposarcoma." Feeling violated, insulted, and in tears I collected my photo envelope and left his office.

By this time in my life, I had health insurance that would pay the bill, so I was not a victim of the system. So I headed back to my GP, who promptly sent me to a second surgeon. This surgeon was the hatchet man and thought it would be great fun attacking my leg. He put me through a couple painful tests while he took more photos then scheduled me for surgery. While sitting in the doctor's waiting room for the instructions for the pre-op, I overheard a conversation. It was with the office nurse and another institution. She was saying: "well he needs instructions on how to perform this surgery, and if he has problems he will Air-Vac the patient to you.

I was the only person in the waiting room, so I knew that call was about me, and I froze. It meant they would start my surgery in Rogers, Arkansas and would fly me to the University of Arkansas in Little Rock in the middle of it should there be a problem. It also meant that I could lose my leg or even my life. Although part of me wanted to be with the love of my life, there was still a part that wanted to stay where I was. The nurse took me into the exam room, and the doctor entered, telling me all the great things he was going to do for me. I asked him, "Have you ever done this surgery?" He responded, "No, but I have done many similar to this, all surgeries are different so this should be no problem." Having the word Blood as part of his last name might make him a great signpost as a surgeon but I was sure my name did not include Guinea pig. I stood; with my hand on the doorknob for instant escape, I said, "Because I do not consider you qualified to do my surgery, you are fired, so cancel my surgery.

I was feeling proud of myself but likewise feeling like a whipped pup, I managed to drag myself home. By now my leg was so large I had to wear sweatpants and walk with two canes. Just imagine you have a pregnancy in your thigh that developed from three months to a full term in 60 days. If this were continued, at this rate, I would be totally immobile in less than six months. From where I sat it seemed that no one knew what to do or how to do it, and I was not sure anyone even cared.

The coldest part of the year was ahead of me, and I was

alone with just the animals. I was getting to the point that it was hard to do anything, except feel sorry for myself. I was full of doubts and depressions as I sat on Kathy's bench in front of her honky-tonk piano and pretended, I could play it. Even chopsticks sounded horrible. She was the life of any party when she played Honkey Tonk music. I had my very own Joanne Castle anytime I brought home a six-pack. The little devil on the right shoulder whispered in my ear saying. "I know you don't drink beer, but Kathy played best when she drank her beer, and there is some left in the refrigerator, try one and see."

I stood up and took a long look around my living room concentrating on the exact details of everything before me. We purchased land with the 100-year-old cabin on it, in the past six years we managed to remodel it into a Tudor style country cottage. I appreciated every detail in front of me as every inch of it has her personality with all its stories that will keep my future active and her image alive. That is if I have a future. I asked myself what she thought the last time she shared this view? The little devil was shouting at me now, "Go get a beer and stop worrying about it." So I did.

I can't tolerate the taste of beer, but it was cold, so I chug-a-lugged half of it. I sat the can on the corner of the piano next to a small box. It was gift-wrapped in party paper, complete with a corsage that included a red rose. It was a party all right, just the way Kathy liked them, and she was fashionable, dressed fit for a prom.

The local steak house was our favorite place to dine out, and so it was the obvious place to have a WAKE. Isn't it? I called and reserved the main dining room for a party of 13 without even questioning the guest list. She looked very impressive as I seated her at the head of the table. To the unaware she looked like a special gift to a lucky person on a special day. Well, I guess I was that lucky person that had enjoyed that special gift for the past 14 years. I choked back a tear that watered her memories.

The waiters were told not to remove empty beer containers, for they must all go to the head of the table. And by the end of the evening the guests totaled thirteen, and the party box was entirely engulfed in empty beer cans and bottles. I'm quite sure the genie that lived in the box was extremely pleased and gave her blessings. I still wondered what the waiters would think if they had realized they were catering for a Renaissance funeral? And what secrets could Leonardo implant in 'Kathy's Last Supper.'

I picked up the box as I had every day in the past two months and held it tight to my heart. I talked to the energy that was hiding inside, that little Genie ready to escape and grant me all my wishes. After the wilted rose was sufficiently watered with my tears, I placed the box back on the piano top next to the beer saying, "Finish your beer, I'll get my own." So I did.

The second beer did not taste nearly as bad as the first. And the third tasted better, I was ready for another party. I went back to stage one and pretended I could play the piano only this time I invited her to join me as a 'walk in.' I told her, " I'll drive you steer, and I bet together we can play this damn thing." And we did.

Or at least I remember we were doing a good job of it when a knock came at the door. Watch out what you ask for I did say, "a party." It was a casual friend, so I invited her in for a beer. She was there to talk about purchasing Kathy's Stallion. Something to remember, when you need something it will come knocking at your door, and this was proof. In the course of our conversation, I explained my dilemma to her, and she had the perfect solution.

"Let me call my brother," she said, "He works at M. D. Anderson Cancer Clinic in Houston Texas. Perhaps he can tell us how to get you an appointment to see a doctor there. So I did, and they did, and I am eternally grateful to this person.

I was an instant candidate and thanks to them; I still have both of my legs and survived the Big "C" with only a 12-

inch scar, perpetual pain, and a lifetime limp. But it is the surgeon's statement that has echoed through the shadows of time and haunted my life from that day. He said, "Within two years it will be back in your leg, and if not there, it could be in your lung or your brain."

For the next two years, they took CTs of my leg every six months. Along with other tests that found tumors in the uterus that were removed, they found cysts on the kidney and tumor on the thyroid along with enlarged lymph nodes in the chest and neck. Several were biopsied along with PET scans while most were put under observation. Somehow over time many of them have miraculously disappeared.

This miracle could have been something as simple as a procedure I performed on myself at the start of each new day. Or maybe without doing anything they would have disappeared. Or maybe without doing anything I was programmed to go with Kathy.

I am the Bull Headed Taurus with ideas of my own, so, needless to say, the Aries side of my sign took over, and I was determined to be in control. With a background in metaphysics including a vast library in my head, I arranged a serious discussion with me myself and I, now considered to be a Council of one. It unanimously agreed that since I was still here, I better make the best of it. So we shuffled through the volumes of gray matter on my shoulders and focused on several facts. First I had to be responsible for my well being since unknowingly I made myself sick, knowingly I had to fix the problem. Realizing, of course, if my mind was powerful enough to make myself sick, then it must be powerful enough to make me well.

Seven years prior I had a stroke involving a near-death experience. To recover from that, I choreographed a procedure that I practiced daily during and after my morning shower. It involved the use of the techniques of visualization and meditation and self-hypnosis.

I choose to perform this in the shower because of the power of "the ION effect." Ions are in the air you breath. They are atoms and are both negative and positive, however it is a negative ion that is most beneficial to good health as it increases the flow of oxygen to the body and brain. It also neutralizes free radicals and enhances the immune system. Negative ions are produced in nature in abundance especially around waterfalls, in front of caves, at the ocean beach, places where water and air mix and in your home this would, of course, be your shower. This unique therapy utilizes air ions as a non-pharmaceutical treatment for wellness. Ions are odorless, tasteless, and invisible molecules. Inhaling them is believed to produce biochemical results once they enter our bloodstream. They increase levels of serotonin, which alleviates depression while boosting energy levels. For most people taking a shower is invigorating. While taking a bath is relaxing, it can often be draining. That is the reason I have not taken a bath in 30 years.

My mind is programmed to think, Body, Mind, and Soul so why reprogram that? So, I take my shower, which cleanses the body, then it's time to work on the mind. I adjusted the water to a comfortable temperature; personally, I like it as hot as possible without burning, perhaps equating it to the shamanistic practice of a sweat lodge. With feet flat on the shower floor and back to the showerhead, I shut my eyes and focus on the top of my head while incorporating all my senses possible.

So I can feel the hot water. I can hear the waterfall. I can taste the minerals in the water. I can smell the sulfur from my well and now with my mind's eye I visualize the water as it hits the top of my head. I watch as it penetrates my entire body collecting debris as it exited the bottom of my feet. I could see it travel through all my body parts my vascular system down to the smallest cells extracting only the polluted particles and flushing them down the drain. Once I feel comfortable that this was completed, I visualized the liquid rainbow of promise following the water through my body to vitalize all my cells with new energy, vitality and wholeness. Knowing that I had taken a giant step in making my health better and my life worthwhile, I exited my shower and went on with my day.

Each phase is not a replacement program; it became an expansion process. Of course, it makes my shower a little lengthy but worth the few extra minutes. Just because I practice my exercises in the shower does not mean that the shower is the only place to create this magic. The magic of visualization coupled with meditation enforced by self-hypnosis is a powerful magic that will work anywhere. I just find in my case it functions best in the shower for being a creature of habit, it's built into a perpetual pattern, so I don't forget to do it. My shower is my trigger to the auto response of singing to myself.

As a reminder, it is important to be aware of, but not to dwell on, while performing this procedure you should incorporate as many of your senses as possible. This way you get your entire body as well as most of your brain involved in your healing program. See the chapter on Senses.

CHAPTER THREE

Phase Three Healing Technique

It is June 26th, 2005, a good day to be alive. It is the 10th day of my third life, and I am on my way home from the hospital. I feel as helpless as a newborn as I observe with renewed awareness all the familiarities of my old life. Once you taste death, you look at life through different eyes, so since this was my second taste, I am now wearing bifocals to view my new world. I knew I had returned from death, but I felt unconformable, crooked in my egg. Just out of touch with my real self, and I could not manage to get my act together. I could hear the voice in my head saying, "The operation was successful, but the patient died." What did my head mean? Was I, really dead and just thought I was alive? Was I alive waiting to die again from an after effect of the surgery? My head was driving me crazy because it would not shut up. "The operation was successful, but the patient died."

It was on June 16, 2005, that I died that second time. The first time was in 1985, at age 46. I had a stroke, and I required a pacemaker to keep me alive. Three pacemakers later and needing the fourth there was no more room in my heart for new wires, so something had to go. The old wires had to be removed to make room for the new ones. That sounds simple BUT.........

My pacemakers have always been a devices with two leads. That means it requires two wires into the heart to function properly. To install the pacemaker, the surgeon created a pocket in my upper chest, just under my collarbone to house the pacing implant. Then he inserted two wires, referred to as leads, through the internal jugular vein giving the lead a straight line to the right atrium. The wires were then guided along the vein and into the correct chamber of my heart. In the first pacemaker, the lower lead was then anchored to the wall of my heart with a small hook. Twenty years later it will be the cause of my dark death. After the wires are in place, the other end is connected to the pacemaker.

At age 52 I required the installation of my second pacemaker. My existing wires did not match the new pacemaker, so I needed a new set of wires inserted into the same vein that was already housing the first two. Things were getting crowded, and that would have been fine, BUT..... The standard procedure, in this case, required the existing wires to be disconnected from the old pacemaker. They are to be tied to the chest wall so they are just there and cannot move or interfere. Somehow this part of the procedure did not happen, so my old wires were left to work their way down into the chambers of my heart. Seeing my heart on a scan looked like a K-9 case of heartworms.

At age 59 my third pacemaker was installed utilizing the second set of wires. Four years later the pacemaker manufacturer recalled my pacemaker wires making my life into a nightmare story. As long as the wires functioned properly they were maintained as usual, BUT....., of course, that was not my luck.

If an automobile manufacturer recalls a defective part, it's a simple process. You drive into the dealership and have it replaced. However, what are you going to do when the part was implanted, in your heart, inside your body? To start with, you are going to lose a lot of sleep worrying about it. Then you are going to have nightmares over the 'what if's' and you are going to pray that you were one of the lucky ones that did not get a defective wire.

I guess I worried too much and did not pray enough. I magnetized my dilemma and at age 64 the defective wires became a problem. It required that one of my two wires had to be turned off resulting in additional problems that eventually at age 65 required a surgery called lead extraction. Of course, the medical profession is not going to inform you of the severity of this surgery. Research information says it is a serious surgery, my surgeon said he had done many of them but refused to answer how many survivors he had. The representative of the pacemaker company would not answer my questions either. But he did say, "Without the surgery, you're lucky to live five years. With the surgery, you probably will probably have twenty." Of course, he neglected to add, "If you survived the surgery."

The surgery is accomplished with a laser instrument something like a soda straw. Disconnecting the lead from the pacemaker, it is then threaded into the straw, and the procedure begins. The straw is walked down your jugular vein, following the wire into your heart. That sounds simple, but if you have ever wrapped a wire around a tree or even hung a swing in a tree you will know that the tree will grow in time, grow to embed the attached object. Your body acts the same as the tree, and it engulfs any foreign object, in this case, the wire going to your heart. Then the heart also engulfs objects; so, got the picture?

That was the day that made its historical stamp on my life, June 16, 2005. I went to surgery, where I spent over 6 hours, more or less. Plus the time I was in limbo, the other side, heaven or hell, or what you wish to call the place you intend going after death. I straight lined on the table during surgery requiring an emergency invasive procedure.

When installed, the wires are often anchored into the inner wall of your heart to guarantee that it stays where it should be. When this wire came out of my heart, it took a chunk of the heart wall with it. That is what happened and at that time I went to zero Blood Pressure. Only by the trained hand of an experienced surgeon and his team of expert helpers was my heart plucked from my chest and repaired. According to my nurse, it took only 90 seconds to crack my chest, exposing my damaged heart. I was then placed on life support while repairs were made; my heart was then paddled, in hopes I answered the call.

In the past, I had requested and received my old pacemakers. This time was no different, and when they presented it to me, it had part of the inside of my heart attached. So, I know for a certainty that the piece that was plucked from the inside my heart was about the size of a kernel of corn. I might be morbid, but I boast of my collection of used body hardware.

That voice in my head became voices, a choir that haunted me continually. I was losing it, maybe the song they sang was true. Maybe I was at the point of postpartum depression. I had not given birth to a child, but I had given rebirth to myself. And I needed to find the child within that was lost in the process. I realized the severity of my condition and knew that I had to do something drastic to take control of my life, or the choir would condemn me. The choir was creating lyrics to the song, 'The operation was successful - oh my God - but the patient died, Ha, ha, ha.'

I have now passed through death's door twice having two totally different near death experiences. The first was in 1985, which was a natural death a White light experience. It was a peaceful death in the warmth of the sun and the energies of cosmos. I was in the presence of the divine creative force; call it God or whatever you wish, as long as you understand that God is energy and not a being. I was light-hearted and happy as I experienced this pleasant life experience. Even death is an experience of the phenomena of life.

The second death was the opposite end of that energy; it was dark and cold and extremely frightening. My memory is not as vivid as it was the first time, perhaps because my body was invaded surgically while under anesthesia. Maybe my spirit got lost trying to escape. I felt that I was wandering in the dark and got pressed against a cold black marble wall. I was helpless because the weight of the world was resting on my chest. There was no hellfire and brimstone, but I could certainly feel the emotion of duality, there cannot be light without darkness, up without down, and life without death. It took over a week to get off that black wall and then I was not too sure that I would come back in one piece. It took over six months for the echoes to stop ringing in my ears 'The operation was successful, but the patient died.'

My recovery was extremely slow, and my body was showing signs of deterioration. My feet and hands were numb, and my energy level was next door to nothing. Half the time, I looked like the blue lady because of poor circulation. In therapy, I was picking up marbles with my toes and Cheerios with my fingers but that was not very exciting, and I didn't need that kind of therapy. I had to do something for myself.

It was back to meditation and visualization only this time; I started talking to myself in a loud voice to crowd out the voices that try to monopolize the conversation. I had the misconception that talking to myself meant that I was senile when in fact I knew I was not. I have been talking to myself most of my life, but this time was different because it seemed to comfort me. It was like a natural tranquilizer to hear my voice. Seemingly, I had found a lost friend in which to confide. Perhaps it was the same friend I talked to as a child in the 40's; the one I saw when no one else could. The one that looked like a Leprechaun. The one that taught me how to hypnotize my father's chickens and my mother's cat and showed me that God lived in nature and not in the church. The one who answered my questions when the preacher couldn't? Questions like "Where did the actually Bible come from?" and "What was the difference between the games God plays, and Simple Simon says?" The one who showed me how to turn my needle and thread, into a dowsing instrument for fortune telling? Grandma reads tea leaves why couldn't I read the dowser? I guess it was that she did it for fun, and I took it seriously.

In meditation, my concentration was focused on healing

the 12-inch scar that marked my chest. To think about the scar was to think about what I knew caused that scar, and it scared the crap out of me. Visualization was much easier. I saw myself as the caterpillar that just cracked its chrysalis in the act of becoming resurrected as the beautiful butterfly. It let my mind ground itself, but the body needed much more than that. The strongest thing you possess is not your body it's your mind, so by controlling your mind you can control your body.

So, my logic and reason kicked into action, and I considered different ways to exercise; for my feet I purchased a treadmill and for my hands, I would teach myself how to play guitar. Of course, you could not have a guitar without singing to yourself, so I started singing to myself. I tried the acoustic guitar, but the neck was too fat for my hands, so I got an electric guitar complete with a speaker and a mike and launched my  career in singing to myself. The more I sang, the better I felt, the better I felt, the more I sang. When I took a walk, I sang to the birds. I went to my cave and sang to Mother Earth. I even got brave enough to sing for some of my friends and a couple times even considered karaoke. It did not matter that I did not have a singing voice because the important thing was that it was my voice, and I was listening to it.

My voice knew how to revitalize me, giving back my energy. It was about this time that I kept forgetting things like; did I lock the door? Did I put the dogs out? Did I turn off the coffee pot? Did I turn off the bathroom light? Did I take my pills, or where did I put the car keys? So, I started talking to myself, telling myself what I was doing. I soon realized that if I told myself something I remembered what I heard. So by talking to myself I improved my memory. By singing to myself, I started feeling better. Logically there must be a magical link here.

Being a creature of curiosity with a mind that would not shut up and a brain that is always hungry for knowledge, I went looking for answers but didn't find much. In just the past few years, the Internet has become a wealth of information, which expands daily, and this is great. What I did find was an educational system called, The Teaching Company, "Great Courses." I canceled my Dish TV as it was boring and put my money into videos that expanded the quality of my brain, improved my self-image and Thought Power. From 2006 to now I've spent my spare time fertilizing my Brain Parts with a continuous flow of college courses. In 2013, I completed the level one and level two Quantum Healing Hypnosis Therapy courses, taught by the world renowned, late, Dolores Cannon. Then in 2014 I graduated from HMI.

In 2015, I will publish this book. The book is dedicated to the late Kathleen Lee, and I plan to release it on her birthday Sept 25/2015.

With a background in Metaphysical Sciences, and the knowing I received as a great gift for dying twice, I sprinkle these pages with the bits and pieces of who I think I am. I offer due respect to all the professors and teachers that have influenced that picture.

In the past, the medical profession was totally oblivious to my real problem, so they disguised the issue with the installation of a pacemaker to keep my heart beating. I knew I had to help myself, and my healing tools of choice were meditation, visualization and self-hypnosis, involving mind and body control. In the years since, I have watched the medical profession implement and develop these same principles with different labels and title it biofeedback. My title is Phase One, Two, Three.

The mind can change the body to fit its natural blueprint, and redesign it, past the limits of your imagination. My compulsive drive propelled me to know and understand why my exercises in self-healing worked. The truth is you don't have to know how it works, just accept that it does.

Everyone has a story, although not everyone is willing to tell their story. Often with the assumption that it only has meaning to themselves, and no one else would care. It is important to recognize that the cumulative experiences of mankind enhance the growth of global consciousness and thus ensure our existence for future generations.

In today's time and space, our planet is changing into new dimensions giving our mind more control over its environment as we realize we possess unrefined abilities. These abilities go along with the technique of singing yourself well. We must view ourselves with renewed appreciation and realize that we are self-sufficient. To get the job done right you must do it yourself, and that is the basic law I used to sing myself well.

You can listen to music all day and appreciate the value of lyrics and sound, although it might be soothing and comforting it is not the healing quality that you need. You can listen to sounds especially orchestrated to match brain wave frequencies, but that is generic in comparison to your voice. The studies of Radionics show you that your personal frequency is as individual as your fingerprint or your face. No sound is going to resonate in harmony with the frequency of your body unless it comes from your body. This special quality makes your voice your personal tranquilizer and instrument of healing. When you talk to yourself, you can solve your problems because you're your best listener. However, by talking, you are using the left hemisphere of your brain, and although you can reason with a problem-solving logic, it is not going to heal you. To come in contact with the magic that heals your body, you must sing to yourself. Singing occupies the right hemisphere of the brain that controls the blueprint of your anatomy and can correct any malfunctions.

I would like for you to consider why does a mother sings a lullaby, why you learn your alphabet by singing it, why do religions sing hymns to God. Could it be that mother's voice is a tranquilizer, singing reinforces memory making. Could chanting and singing be a hypnotic religious drug? A chant is a rhythmic speech that when accelerated becomes a song without words. Your brain views the chant, as common speech equating it with the function of the left hemisphere. When it becomes music, it resides in the right hemisphere and is the magic of the chant. The right hemisphere of the brain opens many doors to your inner self and is part of the magic hidden in ancient teachings of mysticism.

Chanting may range from a simple melody to a highly complex musical score, and it can be chanted or sung without words. It is used to replicate the cosmic music of the spheres, which resonates its wordless Symphony. Based on our personal frequency, we write our prescription for a healthy body. We put our words to our music or sounds and sing them to ourselves. We instruct ourselves on what we wish to accomplish.

The Secret of Phase Two is improving the tools of visualization and meditation plus the powerful tool of self-hypnosis. Visualization is calling on the mind's eye or presenting to the mind the idea that it can convert into an image by using imagination. This image, once captured, can be manifested in physical form by thought and action. Meditation is deliberately focusing on the mind with single-minded concentration. It aligns your energy centers and opens the door that permits magic to happen.

For many years I have approached my audiences with my pearls of wisdom and learn that the resistance to truth is greater than the acceptance of it, so my exuberance lost part of its motivation until now.

"Rule your Mind or it will Rule you." Buddha.

I am ALIVE, and my mission is reawakened to present day issues. So, I will do my best to explain in simple terms the secrets of your universe within, as I know it. To be healed or to be cured of any disorder or disease is not the same thing. This book does not promise you either. It gives you an Alternative way to live if you choose. Along with something to think about and the possibility that my ideas can also work for you. I have no medical authority and have full respect for those that do. In this book, I show you what I have done for myself and what rewards I received. I tell you why I made the decisions, I am not telling you to do as I do but if you choose to you are totally responsible for all your decisions and actions. It's all up to you. Differing belief structures give titles and prefixes to levels of authority, but I accept none but that of open-mindedness, sincerity, and truthfulness. May you accept, for your truth, that part of my truth that feels right to your inner knowing.

"We all start out knowing magic. We are born with whirlwinds, forest fires, and comets inside us. We are born able to sing to birds and read the clouds and see our destiny in grains of sand. But then we get the magic educated right out of our souls. We get it churched out, spanked out, washed out, and combed out. We get put on the straight and narrow path and told to be responsible. told to act our age. Told to grow up, for God's sake. And you know why we were told that? Because the people doing the telling were afraid of our wildness and youth, and because the magic we knew made them ashamed and sad of what they'd allowed to wither in themselves." Robert R. McCammon

CHAPTER FOUR

The Procedure Condensed Version

This exercise is what I consider to be a 1-2-3 process. It was developed in three phases in the process of growth over the period of thirty years. I did not discontinue one process to substitute it with a newer one. Phase One was from 1985 to 1991. Then I was forced to elaborate on the existing exercise, which gave birth to Phase Two, which went from 1992 to 2005. From 2005 until now the process has been evolving into what I referred to as Phase Three.

It means that my showers have become longer over the years, but well worth the extra time involved. Just because I practice my morning exercise in the shower does not mean that this is the only place to create this magic. The magic of visualization coupled with meditation, reinforced by self-hypnosis, is a powerful magic that will work anywhere. I just find it functions best for me in the shower, because being a creature of habit it has become part of my memory pattern. That way I don't forget my treatment.

It is human nature that once you start feeling better you will forget what magic created your wellness. Not feeling well is a reminder to do something about it, like taking a pill for a headache. Well, we are going to label this a preventative medication that you prescribe for yourself and in doing that it is important to make an appointment with yourself every day to do your healing exercise. Don't just read the book and think it has the magic to make you well. It is only an instruction manual, but you have the magic to make yourself well. Like all things that are worth having, you must work for it. You were given the ability; now it's up to you to practice and remember there is no way to overdose on meditation, visualization, or self-hypnosis.

It is important to remember while doing this procedure that you should incorporate as many of your sense as possible. This way you get your entire body involved in healing down to your smallest cells. Every cell in your body has its individualized consciousness referred to as cellular consciousness. They are each living entities that seek to perform their predestined responsibilities. By talking or singing to yourselves, you can improve the activity at the location of the cells you are addressing. For example: if you have a liver issue then talk or sing to your liver cells. Create a liver song.

The entire process is rather simple, I will explain step-by-step the way I go about it. Once you get familiar with the standard idea of how, create your songs and know that the system works. It will be simple for you to create your personal lyrics to address your specialized problem.

In this chapter, I purposely avoid complicated details on theory and ideas. You will find that in the remaining chapters. However, if you are not familiar with meditation, visualization, and self-hypnosis, you might want to advance to those chapters, to improve your skills then return to this chapter.

This presentation is formatted, on health issues, but it can be on anything you want, or any way you wish to change your life. The classic statement is, "health, wealth and happiness." Health being first assumes it is the most important because, without health, the other two are less likely to exist or have proper meaning.

I am going to send you to places to bring back assistance. I arrange my health around rebuilding my body, so I go to my prenatal state and collect stem cells. I sometimes go into the cosmos and collect energy, or into my past and collect memories. I go to my future, to collect goals. In my shower, I collect my pain and send it down the drain. Your mind can go anywhere and can collect any substance you need or think you need to accomplish the task you have assigned it.

You can collect it from anywhere, and you can likewise

deliver to anywhere. I collect stem cells from my fetal state and deliver them to assigned body parts. I often collect understanding and deliver it to my mental library or my emotional self. I collect energy and deliver it to my point of stress. If I am over-energized and antsy, I redirect that energy to other places. It is important that you understand the program, and that the power is limited only by your imagination.

This process can be executed, at any time from anyplace. Take a nature walk and collect life essence from everything you see. Not what you are looking at, but what you 'see.' I see the birds and utilize their magic of flight to lift my spirit, their visual perspective to expand and improve my viewpoint on life. I watch the Bee visit the flowers and collect pollen that it magically converts into life-giving honey, giving me confidence that I can do the same with new ideas in my life.

I examine the vegetation under my feet and focus on just one blade of grass, to test the Buddha's theory that you can hear it grow. I hear the sounds of running water while spotting a frog that leaped into the water, knowing that I have to be brave enough to take a leap into my imagination to achieve my goals. I look deep into the water, past the surface and see other life forms and realize we share the common need for water. I could write a book just about of my walk through nature, but I hope you have the picture on how to approach this project.

Now let's get started; find the most inspirational room in your house.

Find a time and place where you can give yourself all your attention. Avoid any possible interference and do not get too comfortable or you might just fall asleep.

In my case, it is the bathroom. In that one room, I am a captive audience of myself, and it's where inspiration comes in spontaneously as eliminations go out. You might think that strange, but I have received my most creative inspiration while sitting on my throne or taking a shower. It is a place where you can empty your mind while you take advantage of your body.  You need to have the luxury of concentration and focus.

While taking my shower, I continually sing to myself. At this time, the lyrics are simple because my attention focuses on cleaning body parts. It is, a mundane process and utilizes mostly left brain activity as it is accomplished by rote and has no creative intent. Much like mumbling to yourself, when your subconscious mind puts you on hold.

Once I have finished with the necessities, it is time to enjoy the water that is splashing its negative ions over my body. I readjust the water to a comfortable temperature; personally, I like it as hot as possible without burning, perhaps equating to the shamanistic practice of a sweat lodge, and then I begin my deliberate routine. With my back to the wall and the showerhead directly over my head, I cross my arms, hold my back as straight as possible and feel the water hit against the top of my head. I now try to incorporate all my senses. I can feel the hot water. I can hear the waterfall. I can taste the minerals in the water. I can smell the sulfur from my well. My mind's eye can see the water hitting the top of my head and penetrating my entire body collecting debris as it exited the bottom of my feet. It feels great, and now I take more control as I pause and take several deep breaths. The steam is like a vaporizer as I breathe in its power. With my eyes shut, I visualize the water as it enters the top of my head; see it circulating through my body, removing unwanted debris. I direct the cleansing power through the vascular system, the organs, and then the intestinal tract. If I have certain locations that happen to be bothering me at the time, like maybe my back or my neck, I spend more time there. If needed, I visualize incorporating a larger tool, like maybe a pressure washer to clean the stubborn junk from difficult locations. I target the areas that I think need special attention. Then, I tell my subconscious mind to clean up the mess, to detail my project.

Having located and collected all the junk, contaminated cells, and drones, I flush it all down the drain. Watch the water as it goes down the drain because it often contains more dirt than you thought your body contained. Using a syringe, I collected water from my shower before it went down the drain and viewed it under my microscope. It is speckled with reddish brown blood spots. Seemingly, the practice forced impurities through the pores of my skin. I mentally ushered the trash to the bottom of my feet and sing it on its way down the drain. Singing "down the drain with all my pain, down the drain with all my pain, down the drain with all my pain." I sing it three times, to ensure that my inner child is listening to me. Then I get ready for the main event.

Feeling good about getting rid of all the extra toxins by focusing and visualizing them removed from my body, I reinforce my stand, take several deep breaths and start the next phase. I shut my eyes and focus on them at the center of my forehead where my pineal gland has provided me with a TV screen. I see myself the way I want to be, twenty years younger, knowing what I know now and in perfect health. Now I start singing my foundation song, directing it to myself, understanding that it is my conscious mind, sending my subconscious mind to do an errand that will benefit both. Understanding that the subconscious mind is obedient to the conscious mind, it goes like this, Sing:

Jeri Lee C.Ht.

I'm Singing in my Right Brain.
Just singing in my Right Brain.
Singing in my Brain.
Go to my fetal, collect stem cells.
Go to my fetal, collect stem cells.
Go to my fetal, collect stem cells.
Bring them to the future, bring them to the now.
Put them in my bloodstream, put them in my heart.
Make my body healthy, make my body well.
Go to my fetal collect stem cells.
Bring them to the future bring them to the now.
Put them in my liver, put them in my back.
Make this body healthy, make this body well.
Go to my fetal collect stem cells.
Bring them to the future, bring them to the now.
Put them in my lungs, put them in my neck.
Make this body healthy, make this body well.

You make up your song, and you get the cells as you see yourself putting them where you need them. Now while you are singing these ideas to yourself one of them may haunt you, and you will start repeating it. So meditate for a moment on that and visualize calming, if you receive any input that comes your way, welcome it as a healing power. It might give you food for thought for the day.

Remember, stem cells are not the only things you can collect and distribute, your selections are limitless. You can overlap chores and events if you choose, you can sing for health, wealth and happiness all in the same song. I usually work on one thing at a time but your subconscious mind is endless and can multi-task even though your conscious mind cannot.

Now for Phase 3, you must fortify and protect yourself before you leave your temple. Focusing on that TV inside of my forehead, just between the eyebrows, and see with my inner eye. Utilizing this third eye, I relax with three deep breaths then see the White light energy spinning around me as it seals in my current healing session and protects me from all negativity. It might be easier to see yourself inside a light bulb. Once I am comfortable that this is complete, I see the liquid rainbow of promise following the water through my body vitalizing all my cells with new energy, and wholeness as it activates my Kundalini.

This entire process takes only about 5 minutes or less. You will find they are the five most enjoyable minutes of your day. Knowing that I have taken a giant step in making my health better, I exit my shower and go about my day.

If I do my shower before going to bed, I lay in bed and visualize a bright pyramid, well lite with rainbow colors over my bed. I sleep in the protective power of one of the most powerful symbols of Antiquity.

Over the years, this has become a traditional part of my morning, and it is my belief that this simple practice has kept the cancer cells from reoccurring as predicted by my surgeon in 1992. It has kept Lupus, which was the hitchhiker to the stroke 1985, from devouring my life essence, it has prevented other menacing problems from occurring while at the same time healing me from residual side effects.

Let's take a minute here and analyze your first song; you told your subconscious mind what you expected it to do. You then told it three times because that is the language of the subconscious. It is like a six-year-old child. The first time, it says, " OK" The second, it says, " I will think

about it," but the third, it says, "OK, I HEARD YA! I'll do it." Then tell your subconscious mind what your wishes are and repeat it three times. Follow it through, and it will get results. You must remember your subconscious does not have thinking abilities, but it is obedient to the thinking processes of the conscious mind. Treat your subconscious mind like your faithful pet, train it properly, and it will serve you well, untrained it plays all day. For more about minds see that chapter.

Every day when the weather serves me well I take my 21-speed bicycle for a ride. I ride about 3 to 5 miles in the country by myself, which is another great time and place to sing. So I sing to myself. If I do not take a ride, I use my treadmill and go for a walk. Either way I sing myself another song. The songs you sing are your songs. You sing about what you want, about things you are happy with, about your dreams. You will learn to understand yourself by creating your life songs.

Remember, if you are talking to yourself that is all you are doing, you are using the left brain. It is calming and solves minor issues, but if you want something big accomplished you must shift to the right brain. It is the phone line to the subconscious, and it rings God's phone. You must sing your message so that your God-self will answer. Your song does not have to be poetic or have a special musical composure; it can be something like Rapp. It has to contain your message and be delivered in a musical fashion by you to yourself. It must be your voice, or your subconscious will not answer the phone. Make it up yourself, as you go and then make a joyful noise, and be happy while doing it.

Like this:
JUST SINGING IN THE BRAIN
Just singing in the brain.
Go to my, future and see me well.
Go to my, future and see me well.
Go to my, future and see me well.
Give me, the energy to fulfill this fact.
See me, at 80 peddling my bike.
Give me, the strength to follow this dream.
Give me, the ambition to keep me going.
Give me, new ideas that I must prove.
Give me, the courtesy to share with others.
Give my, respect for their thinking.

Give me, the appreciation for my knowing.
Bring these all together, to see myself.
A reflection of, my cosmic consciousness.
The all that lives within me, you and the world.

You cannot make mistakes because you are only singing to yourself, and you are only talking to yourself and you are the only one that has access to your thought so just sing. The inside of your head is your special room. That place where you can go and not be bothered by anyone or anything. It is the special space where you have sole ownership, so claim it without guilt and be selfish about its contents. Then sing another song:

Go to my, future and see me wealthy.
Go to my, future and see me wise.
Go to my, future and see me successful.
Go search, for reasons to make me wise.
Go see, the plans that make me a success.
Go show, me the ways I can see me wealthy.

The most powerful times of your day are both ends of your sleep. So I like to start the day with my shower song and end it with my meditation song.

JUST SINGING IN THE BRAIN
Singing in the brain.
Go to my, dream world show me things.
Go to my, dream world show me things.

Go to my, dream world show me things.
Bring me, lessons in need to learn.
Bring me, pleasures, I love to get.
Bring me, rest, I need so much.
Bring my, the gift of a new day.
Wake me, up refreshed.
Now I am, going to sing in my head.
Take three deep breaths and relax.
See myself on the top of a stair with 100 steps.
And count myself down into a hypnotic sleep -------

Your body is your personal musical instrument, and it resonates at your individualized frequency; it responds only to your efforts and it is up to you to learn how to play it properly. Too perfect, utilize and benefit from its total potential requires a little work on your behalf. You must want to claim your powers and realize this is a gift you have to go after. It isn't just shipped, by UPS. You are limited only by your imagination as you create ways to help yourself. Here is my challenge to you: Sing, "Go to my past and show me what I did to create my illness."

My Rainbow Song
Go to the rainbow, collect the hues,
All of its colors, from reds to blues.
Put them in by body, that I may use.
Put them in my Chakras, that I might know.
Put them in my Aura, that it might glow.
Put them in the third eye, that I might see .

Jeri Lee C.Ht.

Put them in my voice, that I may sing.
Put them in my heart, that I may feel.
Put them in my feet, that I might understand.
Make my body healthy, keep my body well.

When I was 18 years old, a dear friend gave me this poem, and I have carried it in my wallet for almost 60 years. To it, I added a final line of "I TOOK TIME TO LIVE." as my epithet.

TAKE TIME

Take time to think,
it is the source of power.
Take time to read,
it is the fountain of wisdom.
Take time to play,
it is the secret of perpetual youth.
Take time to pray,
it is the greatest power on earth.
Take time to love and be loved,
it is a God given privilege.
Take time to be friendly,
it's the road to happiness.
Take time to laugh,
it is music to the soul.
Take time to give,
it is too short a day to be selfish.
Take time to work,
it is the price of success.
And YES, I took time to live.

CHAPTER FIVE

Over View

In the first four chapters, we looked at my life and how I developed a technique I use to keep myself on the move. I based it on the habits and theories I have developed in conjunction with my belief structure and educational background along with my personal experiences both physical and non-physical. To make my technique work for you, it is not necessary for you to know how magic works, just that it does. However, it is helpful if you have the basic knowledge of what is going on so your mind can better direct your brain, to instruct your body, as to what it is expected to do. So in the following chapters I will give you the basics on the interaction of body, mind and soul and how you can put yourself in the driver's seat and take control of your body and determine your future.

The first requirement is that you believe in yourself, claim your power and be selfish about it. Ask yourself, " If I'm not in the driver seat, who is?" Your mind is the driver, and your body is the vehicle, so take control and let's go for an intellectual ride.

Second, you must practice the simple basic steps until they become second nature and realize that nature has basic laws that it follows for everything, even if we are not consciously aware of them. Learning to control your body is no different than learning how to play the piano. You can look at that piano all day but unless you sit down and diligently practice, you're never going to master it. Your approach, attitudes, ambitions, and emotions are all going to affect the outcome of your piano practice. Likewise, your future intentions and goals are equated into this formula of success in keeping your body healthy. You must view your body as a refined instrument, finely tuned to cosmic frequencies and capable of producing the Symphony of your soul.

Third, you must know that practicing this technique will help you succeed. *Knowing* is the positive keyword that grants this success. Believing it will work, involves having faith that it will work, without the assurance of knowledge. If you practice properly, it will work regardless of your beliefs as long as you have projected yourself to become healthy, wealthy or wise. The favorite quote of my music teacher was, " practice does not make perfect, perfect practice makes perfect."

It is time to take a look at yourself and ask yourself why

you are ill? You might say, 'I do not want to be sick.' But, in retrospect, being ill might offer you rewards that a healthy body would not grant you. You might be on a form of financial assistance that supports you because you're ill and by becoming well that support disappears. You might not be able to cope with the idea of being responsible for yourself. It could prevent you from becoming well. There are other examples, this is only a reference, you have to analyze your situation and take control.

Accepting full responsibility for yourself means all your actions, also take full credit for your results. As long as you realize that the results were possible because you communicated with your subconscious self who obediently followed the laws of nature. The raindrop is not aware that it is collective conscious, collecting life essence from the recycled atmosphere that innocently hovers above the surface of our planet. It is likewise unaware it will soon be a part of the river, and then the ocean, then another rain drops. But will it be the same raindrop?

The River is not aware that it is made up of rainwater that it must carry downstream. While also supporting the abundant life forms that live in it which, could also include, the fish you had for dinner last night. That fish was not aware that he was going to be part of you and support the life of all the cells in your body. It is all the cycle of life that conforms to the laws of nature without reading an instruction manual.

The cells in your body all have an individual life with a prescribed destination and purpose of being, without the awareness of why they follow the instructions of your subconscious mind. Now for the real magic of the scenario: your conscious thinking mind is the only item in this picture that can harness nature and use it for self-gain. It is the only equation in this reality that contains the substance of logic and reason with the projection of an anticipated consequence. It has the ability of harnessing nature for your gain, either in expanding or enriching your life.

My technique functions on its own once you have trained your mind to control your brain to heal your body. Nature consists of automated reactions to a staged situation. In this case, you stage the situation you want, which is good health, happiness, wealth, or whatever you sang for, and the automated reaction of nature makes it happen. It helps if you understand the physics of nature, then you can reinforce what nature is doing, under your invisible control. The remaining chapters will address every puzzle piece separately so you can put the full picture together and understand how and why you were successful in reaching your goal.

CHAPTER SIX

SELF HYPNOSIS

Wikipedia states that self-hypnosis takes the form of hypnosis, which is carried out using a learned routine. It allows the user to gain self-control over personal matters such as pain management, emotional disorders, anxiety or depression, addictive habits such as overeating or smoking as well as drug abuse. Hypnosis and Self-hypnosis both include a long list of compatible disorders that can be improved by suggestibility. It is quickly becoming an option for allopathic doctors as a useful tool in our modern medical world.

The ingredients for successful self-hypnosis are motivation, relaxation, concentration, and direction. Without proper motivation, it will be impossible to practice self-hypnosis. Not everyone can direct himself or herself into a compromising position or state of mind for self-hypnosis. For those who can, they will find it most rewarding. Like all things worth doing, practice will promote success. So, if you are having problems, keep trying, and success is guaranteed if your intent is focused.

Relaxation is a must, as you cannot hypnotize yourself with distractions in your environment. You must find a place where you are by yourself and can be totally comfortable to enable complete relaxation. It might be if you wake up in the middle of the night, or when you occupy the bathroom. The best way is just to lean back in your favorite recliner and take several deep breaths, shut your eyes and sink into yourself.

Concentration is needed to be able to focus your mind on a single item and to concentrate on it in a meditative state. You must direct that attention to a specific goal as you visualize your success. See yourself having accomplished that goal, feel pride in the accomplishment. Then direct this vision back into your daily life so you can live your success.

During the process of self-hypnosis you are totally conscious, you are in full control and you cannot overdose. You cannot get stuck in a hypnotic state of mind, even though you might like to; it is impossible because sleep is a round trip ticket to the land of reality. Remember you live half of your waking time in some form of self-hypnosis. When you watch TV without being 100% aware of what is going on, or when you do your daily routine while daydreaming. When you are driving and cannot remember passing a certain landmark, you are hypnotized. Self-hypnosis is a natural reality, so just take control of it and apply it to your achievements.

Hypnotherapy is a unique way to deal with your emotions, anxieties, and fears of everyday living. Instead of spending time visiting a psychiatrist you can become your personal therapist by understanding and utilizing the techniques of self-hypnosis. You will achieve success to a higher degree if you focus on doing it for yourself, as opposed to focusing on what a therapist can do for you. We have a misguided belief that it is the doctor or psychiatrist that does the magic that promotes our healing when in truth, it is all up to us.

Self-hypnosis produces immediate results as long as you can believe in yourself. There are patients who spent years going to therapy only to be disappointed in the results obtained. If they had confided in themselves, instead of a psychiatrist, their problems would have been solved in a fraction of the time. It is my sincere belief that by talking to yourself you help yourself. That is not to discount the necessity for professional psychiatrists. It only suggests an alternative that is less invasive, more practical and far less expensive. Of course, when this does not work, then follow your traditional path.

In performing self-hypnosis, you are utilizing first relaxation, second meditation, and third visualization. Once again, we are dealing with a 1-2-3 approach. When your mind visualizes an object or experience, the mind registers it as a reality, and the brain accepts it as if it happened. It means that even though you imagine a situation your brain does not separate it from what you experienced. In this way, hypnosis and self-hypnosis act as a psychological therapy of change, putting you in control of changing your life by reprogramming your memory patterns.

Practicing self-hypnosis is a test of the power of your mind. You must practice diligence with discipline to achieve success. You must realize incubation is a time-consuming experience. Planting a new idea in one's mind requires fertilization and attention. Some have suggested that it takes 21 days to promote a new habit. It is often helpful if you keep a diary that daily lists your thoughts, feelings, and actions. It also stimulates the memory and initiates excitement while performing your self-hypnosis therapy.

To get the best results from your inner self, exercise developing your abilities with your third eye. It is the pineal gland that is shaped exactly like your eyeball without the Iris; it sits under your brain just above your brain stem. It is extremely small but equally powerful. It is the light of your inner mind, and the screen on which you project your dreams. It gives you the ability to see inside yourself and create the results you choose for your life. You may go with the flow, or you may change, it's all up to you.

It is often helpful if you make a recording as you are

talking to yourself through the sessions. It might sometimes reveal to your conscious mind the problems with which you're subconscious is dealing. These problems you might be aware of but may have considered them unimportant, when in fact they are the cores of your distress. In this way, self-hypnosis flushes out psychological toxins.

When talking to yourself avoid using negative words. Avoid the words that create doubt or fear. You need to think positive, promote positive words, positive thoughts, and positive actions. All this will produce positive results.

Your mind only thinks in black and white, yes and no, it has no room for gray. When you think with doubts, fears, maybes or if's, anything that would be considered a 'gray' word your mind automatically makes it black or negative. So, think positively, and speak positively, and then react positively. Learn how to change the wording of your sentence. For example, instead of saying, "I'm afraid I can't lose weight," say, " I know I can lose weight one pound at a time." Instead of saying, "I'm always in pain," say, "My pain is going away." In your statement "I'm always in pain," you invited the pain to stay with you. In the second statement, "my pain is going away," you acknowledge the pain existed, but it is on its way out.

Typically, a hypnotherapist would place you into a state of altered consciousness by the use of an induction. It means that they would talk you into a state of relaxation by having you perform several breathing exercises and focus your attention on solidarity. At that point, they suggest that you find a place within, referred to as your 'inner peace' and a place without that you call your 'sanctuary'. It is up to your conscious mind to find that place in your memory or imagination that is so peaceful and relaxing you could lose yourself. But to break the barrier of the minds you must communicate with all three of them. Contacting your subconscious mind that is the intermediate between your conscious mind and your super-conscious mind provides this ultimate experience. It is this connection that permits you to find the magic and purpose of your being.

While finding that door to your ultimate experience might be exciting, it can be equally devastating because your subconscious mind has no conscience. It only wants to please you the conscious mind, and it does not understand unless you put the meaning in simplified direct suggestions or orders because it takes all of your requests as literal orders. So consider thinking about what you request your subconscious mind to do and be very exact. Example. "Go to my fetal state, collect stem cells, bring them to now, place them in my liver, make my body healthy, make my body well. " These are all positive orders that your subconscious must obey.

You can instruct your subconscious to contact you're super conscious, which is your higher self. Being that it is your God-self does not mean that you have to bow or be intimidated. It means that it is the part of your mind that makes miracles happen. Take control of this part of your mind and apply any name you feel comfortable using. I have names for all the parts of my mind. Since my parents named me Geraldine: That converts like this 'Jeri', is my conscious mind. 'Dean' is my childhood name, and my subconscious name by choice, and the super conscious mind is, "Hey, You."

You had no problem disciplining your child by telling that child to do this or do that or don't do this don't do that. You must deal with your subconscious mind as that little child that lives within, and you must talk to that child as if it were your offspring. Taking control, with authority and advanced learning requires discipline.

It is important to utilize as many of your physical senses as possible in each of your sessions. However, realize you must also activate them on your spiritual planes of existence, for this is where their counterparts reside. Visualizing success while utilizing hypnotherapy is like imprinting a memory from short term to long term. You have to detail it in photographic format and imprint it on your long-term memory. Using your spiritual senses to recognize emotional success improves your physical results.

How to hypnotize yourself:

You may purchase self-hypnosis sessions on any preprogrammed event imaginable. I do not suggest this form of self-hypnosis because it is hypnosis, not self-hypnosis. You are listening to someone else hypnotizing you instead of doing it for yourself. Self-Hypnosis means you do it. You hypnotize yourself by listening to your voice or your mind. This fact is extremely important and often misunderstood.

You may also purchase background music for relaxation; this might be useful as long as it is wordless and implies no suggestions. When you are in total relaxation, your mind is extremely vulnerable and highly suggestible to any message that might be implanted in this type of music or outside interference. Our media has injected subliminal information into our world that your conscious mind misses, but your subconscious mind reads; so for this reason total silence is the best background for self-hypnosis.

YouTube is a simple way of acquiring background music if you choose to use it. You can find it specializing in brainwave frequencies corresponding with the four stages of consciousness: Beta, Alpha, Theta, and Delta. Personally, I'm addicted to YouTube fractionalization and initiate my sessions in self-hypnosis with the relaxation of the color drama and formations of fractals without the sound.

Find a comfortable place where you can relax, preferably recline with your legs elevated. Do not cross your legs, but you may rest your arms comfortably on your body. Be sure you are completely comfortable and can maintain this position for the duration of your session. The average self-hypnotic session should not be longer than 20 minutes.

Take three deep breaths, slowly breathing in through your mouth and out through your nose. Concentrate on relaxing all your muscles with each new breath. Visualize a protective White light illuminating your entire body during the entire session. See this White light as containing the rainbow of shimmering colors and know that it will protect and vitalize you for your entire session. As you continue to breathe slowly in and out, you are relaxing any tension and releasing all anxieties. You will be tempted to shut your eyes, so allow them to close as you focus on the purpose of your session.

Just let yourself float on the clouds of thought as they enter into your mind and gently release themselves. Concentrate only on targeting your session. Remember that you are protected, you have no problems, no fears, and you are in total harmony with yourself and the oneness of all. All your body tensions and stresses have melted away, and you have a pleasant feeling of total relaxation. You are in your safe place, so take a deep breath and feel the warmth surrounding your body. Now starting at the bottom of your feet and working to the top of your head concentrate on relaxing every muscle. If you have a physical disorder, spend extra time on that portion of your body while doing this process to relax and energize that area. Spend extra time relaxing your neck and shoulder area and concentrate on your head and brain activity with a focus on your pineal gland and the intentions of activating your third eye.

Once you have obtained total relaxation, you may visualize yourself at the top of a stairway containing 20 steps downward. The bottom of the stairway is the object of your session. Example: if your session is to promote wellness then, you will see yourself as being extremely healthy waiting to meet you at the bottom of your stairway. Then as you step, one step downwards at a time you repeat to yourself an affirmation of health while going deeper and deeper into a trance.

Count your stairs as you ascend to your goals. 19 - I feel great, 18 - I'm totally energetic, 17 - I found the fountain of youth. 16 - life is worth living, 15 - I'm happy with myself, 14 - I love myself, 13- I am creating my new life. Seeing the progression and development of your successful trip down the stairway and acknowledging the challenges as you return to reality will bring awareness to your everyday living and a reminder of your goals. So you can create slogans for the remaining stairs.

At the bottom of the stairway, you embrace yourself and

congratulate yourself for being successful in obtaining your goal. Now it is time to turn and look at your stairway. Then hand-in-hand, you start climbing this stairway as you consummate your union with your projected self.

Once you have obtained success for this session, it is time to come back to reality and realize your affirmation. Since I am in control of my destiny, I know I can have anything I desire. I am relaxed, calm and confident that I will grant my wishes through diligent practice, and I will create a healthy energetic me. So be it.

As you accept your affirmation as a reality, slowly count yourself up from 0 to 5. At zero, you are in your deepest trance so tell yourself to go deeper. Then take a breath in telling yourself; 1 – I am awakening, 2 – I am becoming aware of my environment. 3- I am gaining sensation in my body, 4 – I feel the movement of my eyes, 5 – I am wide-awake, I am wide-awake. 1-2-3-4-5 wide-awake.

Now, open your eyes and relax as you slowly return to full awareness. Take a deep breath then let it out as you sit for a moment collecting yourself and imprinting your new image. Do not be in a hurry to stand and when you do use caution. Work at creating your scripts that follow your ambitions and wishes. Be realistic and do not program a disappointment by asking the impossible. Example: "I want to be a millionaire," and then in a week you will say, "well it did not work." Instead say. " I want to take the first step in becoming a millionaire

PRISONER OF TIME

I am cuffed by life and sentenced to death,
destiny in every breath
My directions of choice was totally mine,
good of bad I am a prisoner of time.
The gridlines I walk are not by chance,
for they are a part of a Cosmic dance.
The rhythms of nature, the riddle of time,
this global footprint is totally mine.
Dharma in Karma out,
this incarnation is my turn about.
I face my past day after day,
good deeds to others is how I pay.
I ended up at the end of the road,
thinking I had cracked the Cosmic code.
I stand in line for my just due,
to find my reward was, 'Finding Myself.'

CHAPTER SEVEN

What is Hypnosis?

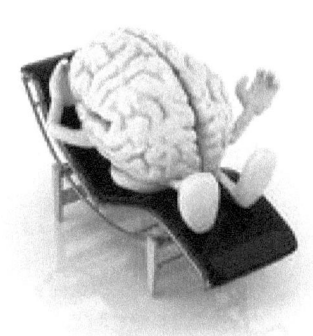

We have already analyzed self-hypnosis and found that it is a normal body function that can be controlled by your mind. The real difference between hypnosis and self-hypnosis is that you are relinquishing your control with hypnosis. Consciously or unconsciously, you are giving permission to an 'administrator' to guide you through the process of hypnosis. This process is historically controversial because it falls in the realm of mysticism. That magic place between knowing and unknowing and not being able to prove. This void between the worlds is shared by many windows of awareness, most of them belonging to our faith-based religious beliefs. Belief and faith are the twins that attempt to harness the truth about these phenomena. They consequently fall into the category of personal opinions, which everyone has their right to judge. This chapter is mostly my opinion on the subject; you're welcome to agree or disagree. It doesn't matter which you choose because, neither way changes the truth; it only adjusts your level of belief

My belief is that hypnosis combines magic with the insights into your inner self. Hypnosis is formless and functions as an elaborate sense through the harmonics of the pituitary and pineal gland. It is not a new item in your anatomy; it has been there since its creation. Evolution has established it as part of the vertebrate system, and in Mesmer's research, he labeled it as a form of animal magnetism. This magnetism is considered magic and the higher evolved animal have more control over it.

As a child, I had no problem hypnotizing my father's chickens, but the family pig was a different story. The pig was more intelligent than the chicken so instead, I taught her to chew my leftover gum while drinking out of a coke bottle. Then I would ride her bareback around the yard while defending her case against being dinner.

Mankind is supposedly the most evolved vertebrate; he has developed this evolution in conjunction with awareness to enable him to take consciously, full control of this magic. I would like to label this other sense as an extrasensory perception, meaning it is a bodily function involving the action and effect of a stimulus on the sense organ of the pineal gland. This gland, being the third eye that gives you the power of looking inward and the luxury of looking everywhere. In my opinion, this holds true in self-hypnosis as well as hypnosis. Understanding this will give you the liberty of being selfish with your power.

History shows that hypnosis has had numerous names along with a complicated and questionable path in acquiring a definition. Some of those names included; Mesmerism, Animal Magnetism, Electric Biology, Human Aura, Mental Electricity, Electrical Psychology, and there are dozens more.

Exactly what hypnosis is still confuses today's scientific world, which questions its authenticity and function, while they discredit its value as a natural phenomena. It falls under the jurisdiction of the medical department, who seemingly want no part of it. Some aspects of psychology recognize its beneficial aspects without the knowledge of its total potential. If you cannot dissect, inspect it under a microscope, weigh, measure, and or inventory it, then it cannot receive the scientific stamp of approval.

The memoirs of the great hypnotherapists in history line the bookshelves of our libraries. My personal library is guilty of collecting a lifetime reference on the subject. In this chapter, we will analyze what others consider the important properties of hypnosis. We will also take a look at how your daily life is controlled by the faces in your environment that perpetually hypnotize you. Most important, I will show you how they do this to you, then how you can own and protect your power. That is important, because if you are not in control, who is?

James Braid [1795-1860] is one or the major figures in the history of hypnotism. There is evidence that hypnosis existed long before Braid, but it lived in the shadows of the occult and mesmerism. Through Brad's insights into the nature of trance and by coining the word "hypnosis" itself, he placed himself in the history books as being the "Father of hypnosis." He used this term as an abbreviation for "neuro-hypnotism." He called it nervous sleep, and he defined it as: "A peculiar condition of the nervous system, induced by a fixed and abstract attention of the mental and visual eye, on one object, not of an exciting nature." Braid elaborated upon this brief definition in a later work, Hypnotic Therapeutics: "The real origin and essence of the hypnotic condition, is the induction of a habit of abstraction or mental concentration, in which, as in reverie or spontaneous abstraction, the powers of the mind are so much engrossed with a single idea or train of thought, as, for the present occasion, to render the individual unconscious of, or indifferently conscious to, all other ideas, impressions, or trains of thought. Hypnotic sleep, therefore, is the very antithesis or opposite mental and physical condition to that which precedes and accompanies common sleep." [Braid]

Until recent years, this method of induction was considered a standard procedure. The hypnotherapist would wave an object in front of the client to isolate the visual attention while; in a controlled voice he instructed them to do his wishes. This object was often a pocket watch or a colored bobble on a chain. It was just anything flashy to be the center of attention, with the objective of emptying the mind of cluttered thoughts.

What is your first response when someone says the word, 'hypnosis?' Most likely it would be, Oh, I can't be hypnotized." Or "You can't make me quack like a duck or walk like a chicken." Hypnosis is one of those mystical words; it contains magic because it is the unknown, and it has the air of suspense. I often hear the comment, "I don't believe in hypnosis", and for them, that means it doesn't exist. Believe it or not does not change the fact that Hypnosis does exist. Many people make reference to hypnosis as being a stage show saying, "That's all phony and full of magician's tricks." Regardless of what you think about the word the fact is, hypnosis exists, and it is a reality. It has always been with us and practiced as part of our human psyche. Like all things in existence, it demands obedience to the laws of nature. These laws are often very simple; it is the overactive ego of humanity that complicates most of them.

Hypnosis is an induction into an altered state of consciousness either self-induced as in self-hypnosis or professionally induced with your permission by a hypnotherapist. You cannot be forced into the state of hypnosis without your permission, either consciously or unconsciously you have to grant that permission. If a therapist has previously hypnotized you and has implanted a keyword, you can be spontaneously re-induced to hypnosis by that same therapist by simply utilizing that keyword.

The misuse of hypnosis in my opinion is using it for entertainment. Although stage hypnosis is the very thing, that highlighted hypnosis into the public eye. The most important use of hypnosis is its value as a medical tool and a focal point of spiritual growth. Its mind controlling abilities historically attracted first the religious institutions then military and medical. Even in today's modern world, that line of hierarchy has not been challenged. All religious faith healers accomplished their magic by using the toolbox of the hypnotherapist. If you analyze their techniques and accomplishments and compare them to a stage hypnotist, you will find remarkable similarities.

The word "Hypnosis" comes from the Greek word Hypnos meaning sleep. In the late 1700 Frank Mesmer referred to this state of consciousness as "Animal Magnetism" Later James Braid, a Scottish physician coined the term "hypnotism" for what he called nervous sleep or "neuro-hypnotism".

The truth of the matter is that hypnosis did not start with Franz Mesmer in the late 1700s, and it didn't even start with Pythagoras in 500 BCE. Man's first natural instinct is and has always been, to be in control, to overpower and influence his environment. Understanding and using hypnosis could grant him this ability. History shows that is was useful in controlling the mind, as in religious beliefs, or of controlling the body, as in a military power.

Ancient Legends shows us how that was accomplished, by such heroes as: Alexander the Great, Jesus of Nazarene, Julius Caesar, Napoleon Bonaparte, Adolf Hitler, Mahatma Gandhi, George Washington, Abraham Lincoln, Winston Churchill and Martin Luther King Jr. to name just a few.

It has always been a recognized fact that prostitution was the oldest female occupation. While history shows that although unrecognized, but well established, hypnosis is the oldest male occupation. According to some references, we can find evidence in the form of sleep temples as far back as 3000 BC in Egypt. I would say, the first recorded therapeutic use of hypnosis was recorded, in Genesis 2:21. "And the Lord God caused a deep sleep to fall upon Adam, and he slept: and he took one of his ribs and closed up the flesh instead thereof." That certainly sounds like hypnosis to me.

It can be stated, with indisputable accuracy that the practice of hypnosis although perhaps known by many other names has its roots in all of our oldest civilizations, cultures, and religions. These practices have progressed through the generations to what we consider to be the modern man. Ancient pictorial Egyptian hieroglyphs demonstrate hypnotic practices along with the ancient Greeks and Romans. This fabric of mind control, in its numerous performances, solidifies the cloak of our unexposed history. The Bible is full of references regarding one individual controlling the mind of another;

these stories, are clearly considered as forms of hypnosis.

Mankind has a history of imprisoning his fellow man by overpowering or outsmarting him to gain control. Hypnosis is an induction through our animal nature and invisibly controls our animal body, both physically and mentally. The spiritual world owns the power of hypnosis; it functions through mind control that is also of the spiritual, not physical world. So by overpowering their opponent both physically and mentally, they become the Supreme.

There has always been a labyrinth of wild speculation and superstitions about the science of hypnotism. Even those interested in developing human knowledge were suspicious of the entangled maze of unanswered questions and confused answers on the subject. The nonscientific investigator was classified, as a 'Quack', in the pursuit of the magic hidden in the unknown levels of hypnosis. It has been the global opportunists who have ventured into the investigation of this tool for the advancement of their personal accomplishments in the evolution of self at the sacrifice of others.

The attraction of these parasites of power was that they did not have to be a physiologist or even have the education to utilize the secrets of hypnosis. The simplicity of this attracted the ordinary laymen and every charlatan that thought it possible to be an entertainer. Because hypnosis was generally associated with the supernatural, it was instantly classified as antichristian making it of the Devil and thus evil. The word hypnosis soon became a by-product of negativity associated with low life, and it's contemptible resources.

To modernize the practice of hypnosis and establish it as a respectable profession required intensive labor on the part of its early pioneers. It was necessary to conquer the superstitions and prejudgment of the person they would eventually label as a client. Even though today's professional world of psychology has tolerated hypnosis as a useful tool, it still views it as part of the 'occult'.

This belief is mirrored in the clairvoyant theories of the soothsayers. It also echoes in the wisdom of the oracles, that predict foresight into the future while the subject tranced into an altered state of consciousness.

The comparison has always maintained a similarity between hallucinogens and hypnotherapy. The question is often asked, is hypnosis similar to the narcotic stimuli without the substance, by utilizing only the mind and its spiritual influence on the brain?

A well knows ancient theory is that the body has the magnetism to heal any disease and illness it might acquire. This follows the concept that if your body was capable of making you ill it is equally capable of healing. Magnetism is a universal agent whose abilities have been recognized by many titles, and when its influence cannot be identified they are labeled as having a satanic implication.

Going back to the Hebrew culture, there is an auto hypnotic aspect of the Jewish Cabbalistic concept from Kavanagh that actually suggests the participation in the practice of hypnosis. Across the globe, these ancient mystical religions regardless of belief structure recognized a hypnotic form of mind control over an audience. This was an obvious factor in the fundamental formation of the Roman Catholic Church that adopted Jewish Scriptures. By following the instructions, "Bow your head, close your eyes and pray to God", you have placed yourself in a submissive position and opened the door to suggestibility. This is the key function on how hypnosis works.

In this state of mind, you are highly suggestible to directions given by the controlling factor, be it you, your therapist or the preacher. This state of consciousness is achieved by creating an overload of message units that triggers the fight/flight mechanism, providing access to the subconscious mind.

The misconception is that a hypnotist induces the clients into a state of hypnosis when in truth the hypnotherapist is a coach that directs a person into hypnotizing himself. Once the client has successfully placed himself or herself in that altered state of consciousness the therapist can easily influence his or her behavior by suggestibility.

The major objective of hypnosis is to establish a connection, a line of communication from the client's conscious mind to the subconscious mind. That introduces a connection from the subconscious to the super conscious mind. It is not possible for the conscious mind to access the super conscious mind on its own without short-circuiting. It needs the go-between of the subconscious mind to achieve that. The conscious mind would be shocked into nothingness if it were to connect directly to the super-conscious mind without the intercession of the subconscious mind. Perhaps the challenge of our future is to be like unto a God having direct communication across this ring past 'not'. [That place in time and space that we do not have the credentials to access.]

In our society hypnosis has many faces. Just because someone does not call himself or herself a hypnotist or a hypnotherapist does not change the fact that they are practicing hypnosis. This list includes anyone that in any way controls or attempts to control or change or modify another's belief or behavior. That would be accomplished, through the influence of one's belief system by creating in them, different ideas and opinions, regardless of their truth. The recipe for this face in the crowd has three main ingredients that are synergistic. To produce this Magical recipe, they have to all be present and work simultaneously.

The first is one-up-man-ship: this means they must take control, they must establish their authority by presenting themselves in a proper costume. That can start with your domestic environment and then go up the social ladder to education, religion, and politics. Look around you and observe in your life those individuals that attempt to take control of most situations. Starting with the school-age bullies that control the playground, to the parents that control their juvenile's life, to the need of keeping up with the "Joneses." Then later, there is the assumption that your doctor knows more about your body than you do. Then the belief in religion, and that the local minister is blessed by God. The police is smarter than you because he has the gun. The soldier is brave because he wears the uniform. The leaders of all these situations are identified by what they wear, the uniform of the day. You instantly recognize the doctor by certain clothing. A politician by a suit, a policeman or military person by his or her uniform, a gun, and a badge, and a judge or a priest by their robes. You take for granted that because they wear the costume, they possess the authority that you assume belongs to that costume. Your mind has been programmed through environmental behavior to respect the uniform they represent. So, without even questioning their credentials you fall into their hypnotherapy trap. That belief structure is so deeply ingrained, in our system from childhood that we are suggestible to whatever demands the owner of that uniform presents to us. Since suggestibility is a precursor to hypnosis, you live your life at the mercy of your pre-programming. The more you learn about how to recognize these social assumptions the faster you can take control of you destiny.

The second ingredient in this recipe is proof of their

authority along with a doctrine: so, the doctor hangs his certificates on his office walls, advertising the great universities he or she attended. These prove to you that they have the abilities they advertise. They rely on the diplomas of the medical institutions they represent to establish their authority. For the same reason, the policeman wears his badge and carries a big club along with a gun. If you do not respect his authority you may instead fear what he is capable of legally doing to you. He is supported by the law and order we live by and represents that illusion. The military person wears stripes on their arm showing what rank they hold over others. They represent our allegiance to that which is worth defending. The judge wears his white collar over his robe and bangs his gravel, showing his authority over our judicial system. His authority is of total justice defended by our constitutional rights. The preacher carries his Bible and claims it is the word of God that gives him the authority to hypnotize you.

For the most part, with their instruments of authority, you never question their authenticity or make them prove their identity because we are programmed to recognize and accept without question certain things in our life. It is especially so, if these people are on their proper stage.

If your doctor is in a medical clinic, he must be a medical doctor and must stand for the required essentials of AMA. He must have the properly required education and be qualified because he occupies the stage of that profession.

In the case of a performer, politician, public speaker, legal judge or religious preacher, the stage is always elevated. That requires you to LOOK UP to these individuals that are looking down at you. That is all part of the psychological profile of one-ups-man-ship. As a child, you are required to look up to your parent because of your small stature and through life you are required to earn the right to look eye to eye at your contemporaries. There have been psychological evaluations to establish the most effective angle of projection from stage to the audience, which gives the speaker maximum control over his congregation.

The third ingredient is you must activate your senses; you must experience something: you must see, hear, smell, taste or touch. When you feel it, you experience an emotion. That is proof to you that something happened. Once you feel something, it becomes real to you as an experience and hypnosis comes alive. The more you are aware of these three tools of natural hypnosis, the better you can control your true self when subjected to public affairs.

Based on your belief structure regarding their qualifications, they are in a position of influencing your life, and that is what environmental hypnosis is all about. Anyone of these individuals, by using these three ingredients can dominate and control another individual or groups by taking advantage of your weakness, with this form of hypnosis. If any one of these ingredients is missing then the magic is gone, because your Spell is broken, and there is an area to insert questions with doubts. Let us say: the doctor was dressed in black leather riding a motorcycle, the preacher was in a bar having a beer, the policeman was sitting on the pond at a fishing hole and a military female was doing a pole dance in a nightclub while the judge was climbing Mount Everest. Do you think this confuses the issue? So, placing these 'faces' in a compromising position unfamiliar to your accepted programming jolts you into a different mental program. You should practice that exercise to reconstruct your identity with your new reality. The first time I told a doctor, "Your fired," his expression was priceless. Realize that doctor is working for you, you hired him to do a job and if he is not qualified than fire him, you have that right.

With these three ingredients, you subconsciously allow a stage filled with hypnotists, to relieve you of the responsible for yourself. They come from the many faces you see daily that you allow to make decisions for you, without even being aware or caring. It is time for you to accept 100% responsibility for everything you are, good, bad or indifferent. Forgive your shortcomings, learn from your mistakes and set goals for you new health, wealth, and happiness.

In conclusion, I remind you that consciously or unconsciously you have given your permission for these 'faces' in your environment to take control and manipulate different areas of your lifestyle. If you had not relinquished your power, they would have no power over you. Today is the first day of your new life. So stand to attention and salute yourself for taking back your power.

Hypnosis is a state of mind that produces a natural trance that can trigger the production of amazing results. It is often successfully utilized in 100's of medical situations. Here is a limited list. Pain; of any type, located anywhere, Addiction; to any abusive substance or action, from overeating, smoking, to alcohol and other drug addictions. Emotional; anger to anxiety, stress, and depression. Physical disorders; cancer, surgery, chemo, child birthing. Ambition: what you want to accomplish, your goals. It is my personal advice to those who avoid the practice: "Try it you might like it.

CHAPTER EIGHT

SB Meditation

What is Meditation? Webster stated, it is to engage in mental exercise [as concentration on one's breathing or repetition of a mantra] for the purpose of reaching a heightened level of spiritual awareness.

A medical dictionary says that meditation is a practice of concentrated focus upon a sound, object, the breath, movement, or attention itself in order to increase awareness of the present moment. This is done to reduce stress, promote relaxation, and enhance personal and spiritual growth.

From Wikipedia: The term meditation refers to a broad variety of practices that include techniques designed to promote relaxation, build internal energy or life force and develop compassion, love, patience, generosity and forgiveness. A particular ambition of meditation aims at effortlessly sustained single-pointed concentration meant to enable its practitioner to enjoy an indestructible sense of well-being while engaging in any life activity.

Meditation is not exotic, it is not dangerous, or an escape from reality. Although it is an exercise, it is not Yoga, it does not belong to the monks, and it is not religious. It is a practice that is beneficial to your personal well being in understanding of yourself. It is used in yoga as well as all religions even though they might not admit it. Many are oblivious to the fact that prayer is an extension of the practice of meditation.

This book is not a teaching guide to meditation; it is only a door opener to what is available, and a few facts for you to consider. There are many information websites as well as 'YouTube' for an endless supply of data on explaining different forms of meditation. Be sure you feel good about the one you choose or go back to the search and push the delete button.

Meditation is an ancient practice that can hypothetically, be traced, over 5,000 years into our past. However, some of the earliest records show that meditation comes from the Hindu traditions [1500 BCE], of Vedantism. As Hinduism merged into Buddhism in the 6th to 5th centuries BCE, many forms of meditation developed, especially out of the Vedas in ancient India. Others developed from Buddhism in Taoist China, and since, differing forms of meditation have been flourishing in every form of religion.

Over the millennia, different styles of meditation have

developed. Each new religious tradition changes it and claims authenticity for their belief structure and their god. Hinduism is credited with being the oldest religious tradition and thus the birthplace of meditation. The three faces of their God are: Brahma as creator, Vishnu as protector, and Shiva as the judge. Much later Christianity changed this system from meditation to prayer and the God hierarchy to; Father Creator, Son protector and Holy Ghost, the judge.

In the Middle Ages, Jewish meditation grew and created changes involving the Kabbalistic practices. This expansion gave birth to a school of thinking supported by Magic and Mysticism. Meditation quickly became their tool of focus in their search for a God of creation and Power of control. Meditative Ecstatic Kabbalah is a branch of the Kabbalah that concerned itself with uniting the individual with God through meditation. The term meditation picked up a second noun and became canonized as a meditative prayer.

Then along came the Christian tradition and picked up the practice of meditation but favored the title of prayer. They harvested the traditions from their ancestors and practiced their version of Judaism, which included the power of meditation, commonly called the power of prayer. They structured their meditation in the form of prayer directed out to God, as opposed to meditation directed into self. Christian prayer is designed to increase your knowledge of Christ whereas Buddhist meditation directs the same energy to finding yourself.

The philosophy of Buddhism is the core of most forms of meditation. It encompasses a wide variety of techniques, and it is credited for, having placed the format on meditation. It is based on the basic fourfold formula of salvation by following the laws of morality. Those laws are: contemplation, concentration, knowledge and liberation. This places meditation as one of the steps on the path of salvation and immortality.

The Buddhist techniques of meditation have become increasingly popular to non-Buddhists. The techniques of Buddhist meditations are designed to develop your concentration, mindfulness, spiritual powers, insight, and tranquility. That might sound simple, but the in-depth philosophy behind each exercise translates into hundreds of different meditations for differing schools of logic and reason. In the Tibetan schools, there are over a thousand visualization meditations alone.

In the past few decades, meditation has become a commercial business under the watchful eye of organizations that are more interested in money than they are in your wellbeing. They charge you membership and counseling fees along with numerous other services. They promote their deception mainly to convert you to their spiritual way of thinking. They become very religious about it to the point of claiming they alone have the magic of the masters and the truth of the cosmos.

Do not be sucked into the popularity and think it is complicated, and you need to spend money to get the thing you need or want. Meditation and prayer are FREE. You do it for yourself and do not need a mediator.

One of the earliest traditions was Zen Buddhism, which taught that there was no exact method of meditation but that all methods should be developed to focus on the development of yourself. The Buddhist path of meditation follows the path to enlightenment with training in virtue, tranquility, and wisdom. Buddhist meditation teaches you to go within to find the best qualities of self-awareness. Christian meditation teaches you not to focus on yourself but rather to focus on the biblical deities and the life of Jesus. Although the Buddhist philosophy is regarded as being free of dogma, it contains many avenues of supernatural powers gained only by enlightenment and persistent practice.

Our world today is experiencing drastic changes through the appreciation of the benefits of meditation and its effect on daily affairs. Healthcare workers along with a growing number of doctors and even medical institutions are looking into the magic of meditation. It is being offered as a possible substitute to the pharmaceutical pill. It has shown itself helpful in all forms of illnesses, either of the body or of mind. Some insurance companies in conjunction with health institutions currently suggest that a patient meditates before going into surgery and visualizes positive outcomes. The types of medications they suggest start with breathing and then focusing on mindful meditation.

The Journal of the American Medical Association suggests that the ancient Eastern practice of mindful meditation can offer real help for patients with depression, anxiety, and pain. Researchers are finding when it comes to the brain, meditation offers greater emotional well being with happier faces and greater emotional resilience.

The biggest problem with the medical world and the practice of meditation is that there are so many types and styles of mediation. Interlace these with belief structures and they all sit comfortably under the umbrella of Meditation and confusion. From this point, it is difficult to prescribe a common term or agreeable understanding. This lack of uniformity proves to be problematic for the medical world.

There are many ways to meditate, to start with keeping it simple is best because it is not complicated unless you make it so. There are likewise several physical positions to put yourself in, namely, walking, sitting, standing or lying. Most important is to be comfortable in the form of your choice to better hold your attention and maintain focus. There are four basic categories that all meditation practices could fall into: Concentration Meditation, Mindfulness, Open Awareness, and Guided meditation.

Meditation has become a fad that topped the popularity list as something you should take seriously. It seems to be the 'in' thing to do but even in a confused state of development it is beneficial to global consciousness. I am only bringing attention to five of the most popular forms of meditation but for more information check the Internet.

Transcendental Meditation
Has become popular by the initials TM and is probably the most popular of modern meditation because it was made famous by the Beatles and the Beach Boys in the 60's and 70's. TM was developed under the guidance of the late Maharishi Mahesh Yogi [1917-2008]. This meditation centers on a single word or mantra for about 20 minutes twice daily. You practice to avoid distractions and promoting relaxation while at the same time being fully aware of your thoughts.

The New York Times states, "Another recent study focusing on transcendental meditation, published in the American Journal of Hypertension, focused on a healthy young population. It found that stressed-out college students improved their mood through TM., and those at risk for hypertension were able to reduce their blood pressure."

Walking Meditation
Walking helps the entire body and gives your brain a chance to move around. You walk around your environment all the time but have you ever observed exactly, what you do when you walk? How your body moves, what makes one foot go in front of the other instead of side by side. What makes you move fast or slow and

how your body reacts to the things around you? When doing walking meditation, your eyes are usually open, you center yourself and focus on your walk that can be short or long but directed to being attentive. It can be a walk in the park, in your yard, or around the block. You can walk back and forth in a straight line or around in a circle. The object is that you are never in a hurry, and you are enjoying the movement of your body with shoulders back, chest out while you walk yourself into thought.

Zen Meditation
It is a seated meditation, on the floor in the traditional lotus position. Keep your back completely straight, head held erect, your mouth closed, eyes lowered as you gaze to the ground a few feet away, you may close your eyes if you choose. Focus your attention on breathing through the nose as you count your breaths. Your jaw is one of your strongest body parts so try to relax it as much as possible without letting it open. Your body should have good posture so visualize a rod of energy holding your back erect while properly aligning your neck and balancing your head.

I like to see that energy rod as a rainbow-colored beam connected to the Cosmos. Relaxing with a smile on your face will put you in a happy mood. If your mind gets adventurous and wants to wander, draw it back into that rainbow by focusing your imagination. Concentrating on relaxation will control mental chatter.

Yoga Meditation

Yoga is a Hindu spiritual and ascetic discipline that has adopted for its specialty, the discipline of specific bodily postures. It has become widely popular in health and exercise programs to promote relaxation.

Coming from the Sanskrit word "yuj" which means "to unite." It is all about using different breathing techniques while assuming yoga body postures in meditation. Through an emphasis on the inner experience of meditation, your aim is to unite body, mind and soul. Life becomes more fulfilling, and you're happier with it when you live in harmony with your environment. Although mostly recognized today as an exercise program, Yoga is an inspirational philosophy and is one of the six major orthodox schools of Hinduism.

Mindfulness Meditation

Now let's look at Mindfulness meditation, which is the skill of being attentive to one's experience as it unfolds. In this practice, your focus is slow motion and deep observation to every detail of the subject being observed. That can be an object or an action, but our interest is to know and understand it completely. It is practiced without judgment or opinion so you must set your ego aside before entering this task. By becoming successful in the practice of mindfulness meditation you develop the twin virtues of wisdom and compassion. It is a moment-by-moment concentration on all things you. Approach it as if you were the observer, outside yourself and you accept, at this time, everything that passes by. Do not attempt to plant thoughts, instead just let them happen. You do this by relaxing as if the thoughts belong to someone else. There is no right or wrong in this practice. You concentrate on being active in the present, being attentive to any changes in body, mind, or soul. You are in the living moment and awake to the experience of deep thought. To practice Mindfulness meditation, sit in a comfortable position keeping your back straight. Close your eyes while paying attention to your abdomen as you breathe in and out. Be aware of your breath; feel it go into your nostrils, and then deep into the lungs. Focus on your targeted project and if other thoughts get in the way, release them and return to your project. Your mind likes to wonder, it's your responsibility to keep it focused. To start with, practice this for about 8 min, and then increase as you practice. Remember you learn to meditate by meditating.

Try this exercise: Space your time for this exercise to last about 8 minutes. Take an orange and a knife to cut it; I am sure you know everything about an orange so this should be easy. Now let's meet Mr. Orange: hold him in your hand and observe that he is round and has an indent in each end. One end looks as though it had been connected to a branch. Visualize that orange hanging on that tree. Wonder about the part of the country where this very orange grew and how it got from there to you. Now notice he has a smooth leathery surface with a slight texturing that feels soft. Slowly roll him around with both hands and see that he is orange in color and cool to the touch. Now slowly lift him to your face while at the same time remembering all the details you have observed to this point.

Take a deep breath and inhale the fragrance of Mr. Orange and notice anything unusual about that smell. Enjoy this aroma for you are enjoying meeting Mr. Orange for the first time, you always thought he was just a fruit. Now it is time to see what he is really, made of so slowly lower him off your face and carefully cut Mr. Orange in half. He now appears quite different, and you analyze the new Mr. Orange, who is now beside himself. Notice that the orange color was only a skin and under that was a white cushion of soft fiber then the juicy part that makes him an orange. Bite into the skin of the orange and analyze the taste, and then the cushion and compare the taste. Once you have decided that it was not the part you wished to eat, you take a bite from the center of the juicy body of Mr. Orange. I know after all that you want to jump into that orange and have a snack but learn control. Break the orange apart and slowly, very slowly suck the juice out and deliberately enjoy each wedge of this juicy fruit. You just performed a mindless meditation.

Next take a situation of concern, a problem, an illness, a goal, in substitute for the orange and do the same slow evaluation. You're learning how to meditate. There are as many schools showing ways to meditate, as there are things to meditate on. Meditation is listening to the small voice within, and you must be silent to hear it. You must intentionally rid your mind of all thoughts of daily activities good or bad and think of nothing. You must be nonjudgmental and open minded to unsolicited information that might cross your path.

Before starting your meditation routine, you need to understand your intention and then focus on that goal and set a scheduled ritual for practicing. I am assuming it is your intention to discover yourself. To recognize your potential, promote wellbeing, and wellness while becoming successful. The ingredients that will make this function are that you are willing and open-minded. Then find the time each day to develop this practice into a habit. Ten to fifteen minutes each day is all that is required to make drastic changes in you life.

If you choose the lotus position, find a comfortable pillow to sit on and place yourself so you can sit erect; do not lean against the wall. You want the energy to flow freely, around your body and through your seven chakras. Sit upright yet relaxed, allowing your blood to flow properly and for you to breathe without obstructions. You can do this same practice if you sit upright in a chair putting your feet flat on the floor. You can also meditate while lying flat on your back, but this can encourage unwanted sleep.

The question is what do I do with my hands? You can just relax them anywhere or you can utilize them in stimulating the flow of energy. If you rest your hands with palms and fingers pointing them up you can collect energy. Focus this energy into your Aura as you surround yourself with White light. Always protect yourself with White light energy before you meditate. This White light can be in any form, a natural geometric shape would be best. My first choice is the shape of a pyramid; I place myself inside the pyramid of bright light. My second choice would be a circle or ball of light, or I sometimes put myself inside a light bulb.

The pyramid is a generator of energy, and the circle is the cosmic oneness, the totality of all. The symbol of the TAROT is the pyramid inside the square with a dot or circle in the center. Total protection, because from above looking down on the pyramid it is a square, the four suites or classes of life. From ground level, it has three sides for the three levels of consciousness of the major arcana. The tip of the pyramid being zero, symbolic of you, 'the fool,' and the cap of the pyramid is equated with reincarnation, your soul and your penal gland.

Meditation has a different meaning in all religions, but the objective is the same. It is to seek an inner self and find the source of creation. In truth, meditation has always walked hand in hand with self-hypnosis, visualization, and prayer.

Google says that a prayer is a solemn request for help or expression of thanks addressed to God or an object of worship. Prayers are asking for something and in clinical tests with photos of the brain it shows that prayer is no different than carrying on a conversation with your friend. When you pray, you are folding your hands, which holds in the energy. To meditate is to think or focus one's mind for a period of time in silent listening. So these photos of the brain show that Prayer is talking and meditation is listening. Praying, you are asking for something whereas in to meditation you are listening for the answer. Since you cannot do two things at the same time, it is impossible to listen if you insist on talking. Let us meditate.

You are in and out of meditation all day long. At the same time, you are vacillating in self-hypnosis. Your subconscious mind likes to drift into itself and space out, but getting lost in a daydream is a mundane form of meditation. These practices happen without any creative thinking and thus belong to the left-brain habits.

Plan your daily routine and allow a certain amount of time for meditation. Make an appointment with yourself to meet in a place of solitude, where you can spend quality time just totally enjoy nothing, or something if you choose. The total time spent in one session may vary but should be some comfortable spot between 15 to 30 minutes. Too much and you might get bored, too little and you might not think it is working. Any constructive meditation you accomplish is beneficial and ending with a happy feeling will make you eager to return the next day. If at all possible make it at the same time, so it becomes a habit. It is more important to practice each day for 10 minutes than it is to do one hour every sixth day. As a child, I was taught to say my prayers before I went to sleep. That was an early indication that this was a good time to talk to whatever power that gave me life.

You are more likely to concentrate on a topic of meditation before you go to sleep than you are when you just wake up. These are your two windows of power; when you are not quite asleep and when you are not totally awake. If you can learn to control yourself at these two power points, you can master meditation. That is the time to remember dreams and set goals. To focus on what is important in your life, what you have overlooked and what you need to accomplish.

For centuries, Meditation has been the tool of the human mind to find the mysteries of life, to talk to the angels and spirits and to observe the wisdom of their Creator. In all philosophies involving what humanity believes as opposed to what nature dictated there are those who attempt to destroy the advancement of a beneficial practice. That is what some Evangelical Christian leaders are attempting as they label the success of meditation, saying, "The embrace of yoga is a symptom of our postmodern spiritual confusion."

"Yoga has become a universal language of spiritual exercise in the United States, crossing many lines of religion and cultures, ... Every day, millions of people practice yoga to improve their health and overall well-being. That's why we're encouraging everyone to take part in PALA [Presidential Active Lifestyle Award], so show your support for Yoga and answer the challenge." – Barack Obama

The Three Faces in my life

They are my three parts
Maid, Matron, Crone.
I was a Virgin; Innocence was my name.
Education was my goal, and maturity was my aim.
The Matron taught me life, how to give and how to take.
How to Mother, how to care.
How to laugh and how to cry.
Now I am the Crone, life's experiences I can share.
It's Wisdom I have to offer; Tolerance I can teach.
It's inabilities I must endure, but It's ALL just me.
Who is there to Listen, who is there to care?
Just me, JUST ME.

CHAPTER NINE
THE PINEAL GLAND

It is early morning, and the sun is about to show its face at the far end of my drive. That master of life, creator of light, and custodian of all growth. Is it any wonder that the Egyptians called the sun 'God' and gave it several names. Ra, being the one I like the best, I greet the sun every morning with three cheers, Ra, Ra, Ra. I relax in my yard chair for 30 minutes each morning while I a bathe in the sun as I collect my vitamin D and drink my coffee. I invite the sun to activate my pineal gland and shine bright into my third eye.

Before you question my motive check the back of your one dollar bills. You see the all-seeing eye and behind it is the bright light waves of the sun. In the language of symbols it says, "Let the sun energize you third eye"

Have you ever given the sun credit for being the only part of our environment that greets every person on this planet every morning? As you look at the sun billions of other people are doing the same thing. The sun sees everything you do, did the Egyptians set in stone things we are not listening to?

The idea is to realize there is an umbilical cord called the golden thread of life that connects you with God energy. This cord comes from the source of energy the 'God Ra,' to your pineal gland. At death, this cord is broken, and you are born into the astral plane of existence.

Your birthright was implanted into your psyche at creation along with all your other body parts and on all levels of existence. Believe it or not, you are a perfect creation, capable of accomplishing mystical feats by just simple applications, like singing to yourself, like talking to yourself, or just creative thinking. You must gain or regain control of your pineal gland.

Our history shows that as a race, we relinquished 'our power' to control the social order, the one that had the biggest stick. It stamped labels on our psyche. Like the words; GUILT, FEAR, PREJUDICE, DOUBT. Chemicals in our food, fluoride in our water and toothpaste and more listed at the end of this chapter. The only thing that sets you free is the addition of the most powerful word in our language, and that is:

Jeri Lee C.Ht.

'TRUTH'
**Truth is lonely; it stands by itself as a solid form,
It is surrounded, by pollution, called personal opinions,
Truth stands alone; Truth shares nothing,
It just is; Truth is Alive.**

It is time that we realized our history is not what we have been led to believe. However, Mother Nature has come to our rescue. In the Age of Aquarius, which started in the mid-1900's and highlighted on 12-21-12 the veil of stupidity lifted from humanity. Those who were capable of understanding higher concepts gained access to instant knowledge by just asking it of self. Part of that wisdom was answering the questions of how and why my technique works.

It is necessary that humanity as a whole becomes aware of their TRUTH and claims their birthright as a total part of the collective unconscious.

The Bee knows how to make honey by instinct, and it builds a hive while the ant aerates the earth and builds a hill. The bee cannot function like an ant and likewise the ant will never produce honey. The Human animal gets to make choices, we can act like the animal kingdom, or we can become the God Within. When you take control of self and use this power, you can move mountains, and you can heal yourself. It all has to start with the pineal gland where our DNA blueprint resides. So start singing in the brain. This chapter is probably the most important chapter in this entire book. And the one I hope will impress my reader enough to research and use caution on the things you allow to get into your body and mind

The pineal gland physically:
The pineal gland is part of the endocrine system, and it was the last to be discovered. Located in the center of the brain, it is a small gland, about 8-12 mm long, about the size if a small bean. It lives in a small cave behind and above the pituitary gland. It swims in a bath of cerebrospinal fluid, which is between your eyes. Located in the third ventricle, it is the only midline brain structure that is unpaired. Unlike some body parts, it has ample blood flow, in the same category as the kidneys.

It is multilayered and shaped resembling a pinecone. Thus, it's name Pine-al. Its job is to produce the hormone melatonin, which is a neurotransmitter that is similar to DMT, which enables you to sleep at night. At the same time, it also produces a small amount of antioxidants. Associated with telepathy and the third eye it is also closely connected with similar responsibilities in the pituitary gland.

This gland is larger in children and decreases with age,

starting at puberty. Some scientific research suggests that this organ was nature's first eye. One of the oldest references to the pineal gland is in the writings of a third-century B.C. Greek physician named Herophilus. He discusses the pinecone shaped organ and estimated it to be about the size of the fingernail of your little finger. Its name comes from the Latin word pinea, which means pinecone.

We have all heard or used the term 'you have rocks in your head' well in some cases this is very true. You do not want to have rocks in your head because that means that your pineal gland is calcifying. This calcification can restrict the gland from functioning properly. Often it is found in Alzheimer's disease and dementia. This calcification contains a build up of Calcium, phosphorus, and fluoride. It is estimated that 40% of our population, have rocks in their heads by the age of 18. Medically these rocks are called "Corpora Arenacea or brain sand."

Suggesting that the pineal gland is a remnant of a much older and larger gland might link our primal memories to stories like Cyclops. The pineal gland is the duplication of our other two eyeballs with one exception; it does not have an iris. The theory is that once upon a time it had an iris, and we used it like we use our eyes today. Another theory is it does not need an iris because it is piezoelectric and produces its form of light, which lights up your body.

In 1980, I met my spirit guide face to face, and he has three eyes. He calls himself 'OM' and has been with me most of my life. I never questioned why my guide appeared male or why he had three eyes. However, I do question everything else and usually get unusual answers.

The pineal gland medically:
You can have Tumors and even Cancer of the pineal gland, but it is extremely rare. If you start controlling the negative influences on your pineal gland, this will never be a threat to you. In 1958, Yale University professor Aaron B. Lerner went to the pineal gland in search for a treatment of skin disorders and found Melatonin. It was not suitable for skin, but like many intentional searches gone awry, it gave birth to his fame and proved useful in understanding what the pineal gland was doing for the body.

The pineal gland Philosophy:
The 17th-century scientist and philosopher, Rene Descartes, did in-depth studies on the pineal gland. He stated that he believed it was the "seat of the soul" and that it connected the physical body and intellectual mind. Since it was the only non-paired part of the brain it had to mean that it was connected with thought because it is impossible to have two thoughts at the same time. That is what all literature states because a brain is a physical form, and thus the scientific world can only dissect and photograph physical parts. They do not see the other part of the pineal. The fact has always been simple to me,

"nature follows the law of simplicity and sameness." If it is a member of the brain club, it must have a partner. So the other part of the Pineal gland is the Mind and the golden cord that connects you to the living and gives you consciousness. The Pineal gland is activated by light and working in harmony with the hypothalamus gland controls the biorhythms of the body. It is your biological clock ticking away on our aging process and sexual drives. It also governs your other appetites such as hunger and thrust.

The Third Eye:
The pineal gland has long been referred to as the third eye. It is related to the Ajna Chakra involved with mystical awakening and enlightenment. It is the home of your highest state of consciousness, giving you clairvoyant abilities and extra sensory perception. Flashes of intuition and sensing are harmonious with the third eye when it is awake. As the pineal gland is in the center of your head, it is correlated to the Pyramid Giza, the largest pyramid located at the center of the planet. This secret is hidden in plain sight on the back of our nation's one-dollar bill.

In Buddhism, the third eye is known as the middle eye of Shiva. In Egyptian it is the eye of Horus or the eye of Osiris. In Hinduism it is the eye of clairvoyance. Medical science calls the pineal glad "the atrophied third eye".

The pineal gland and DMT:
Our bodies produce a small amount of DMT, and the

source of this holozoic genic drug is thought to be the pineal gland. Some researchers suggest that the pineal gland has primitive retinas with dual purposes of capturing images and producing melatonin, dimethyltryptamine, and pinoline.

Since the pineal gland is certainly active when we sleep, I believe the images captured naturally are our Dreams. Then when we learn how to control it with visualization, we can project images into our daydreams. The pineal gland is a photosensitive gland and works in harmony with the hypothalamus. The path between the retinas to the hypothalamus transports information about light and darkness to the pineal gland. When there is no light, the pineal produces melatonin and when there is light the production shuts off. That means if you sleep in a room with a light on you do not get your required production of this important substance. To regain our best health, we should design our life to live in the light and sleep in the dark.

The pineal gland and evolution:
It has been considered by many that the pineal gland is the engine of spiritual evolution, the God Embryo that connects consciousness to matter. Folklore has an expansive mythic tradition that weaves the stories of one eye or three eyes through our literary history.

The Ancient Greek, Galen [130-210CE] calling it by the name glandula pinealis, ascribed it to be the size of a nut in a pinecone, a 'pine-nut'. He claimed it did nothing more than any other gland in the body, to support the flow of blood. Plato called it "the eye of wisdom" and claimed it understood mathematical equations like scared geometry. It may indeed hold the secrets of divine enlightenment.

The pineal gland Vatican:
The Vatican has become very liberal in the past 20 years, but in my childhood the mass was always in Latin, which was not understood by the congratulation. We were forbidden to read the Bible because we might try to interpret it for ourselves. That was not the belief of my family, but it was of my best friend. I was allowed to accompany her to her church, but she could not enter mine without confessing to her priest that she has sinned. Then my mother would tell me that I was going to heaven, but my friend was not because she was a Catholic. None of that made sense to me, but it was part of my journey of finding my truth.

Now I want you to start thinking, so at this time I will ask you several questions. First the Vatican has controlled most of the world for the past 1,500 years, and their number one technique was to keep its members humble, obedient, and brainwashed. So, what have they been hiding from us all this time and Why? Then ask yourself, Why did the Vatican form an army of Crusaders? And what were they really guarding? And why did organizations spring from the Knights of the Crusaders such as the Masons, the Rosicrucian's, the Knights

Templar, the Hermetic Order of The Golden Dawn, and more? Why did the Vatican attempt to destroy all forms of written documents and traditional verbal ceremonies that gave other viewpoints outside their cannon Scripture under their control? Why is the courtyard of the Vatican home to the world's largest pinecone? And why is there a sarcophagus and Obelisk in that same courtyard also as well as in Washington DC and why are the Egyptian pyramid and all-Seeing Eye on our one dollar bill? I could answer all these questions for you, but this book cannot be that large, and I want you to think and research.

The Bible:
The Bible tells parables and stories to show the truths to us. Our ancient ancestors knew the map of the heavens in detail. They had records regarding the planet Pluto before our science recognized its existence. So, what makes you think they did not know the map of the human body as well? Recognition of the workings of the body have only been rediscovered in our time and credited to our modern day scientific community.

Genesis 28: 10-19 Jacob falls asleep and in a dream he saw the ladder that goes from the earth to heaven where the angels were going up and coming down, this has been called the stairway to heaven. I believe this refers to the kundalini so when it is activated you will feel it at the base of the neck at the sixth chakra, the third eye.

Genesis 32: 22-32 KJV These verses describe the scene where Jacob wrestles with a man, believed to be an angel or God in the land of Peniel. He wrestled all night and requested freedom at dawn. I am going to take the liberty of naming the man Melatonin, that is a product of the night. He was wrestling in his head in the pineal gland. When Jacob saw the light, the melatonin stopped, and he asked to be blessed and also stated he had seen the face of God. By the sound and ownership of his name, he was able to see the face of his God. This story is all about the Pineal and lets you see a picture of your interaction with this gland. Memory dictates that if you put anything in a photo form you will remember it, as a picture is worth a thousand words.

Mathew 6:22 "The light of the body is the eye: if therefore thine eye be single, thy whole body shall be full of light." KJV

Luke 11:34-35 "The light of the body is the eye: therefore when thine eye is single, thy whole body also is full of light, but when thine eye is evil, thy body also is full of darkness. Take heed therefore that the light that is in thee be not darkness.

An ancient Egyptian proverb says, "The Kingdom of Heaven is within you and whosoever shall know themselves shall find it." Pythagoras is noted as saying, "Man know thyself."

REACTIVATING THE PINEAL GLAND:
Before you get all upset that your pineal gland is shot, and you can not reactivate it just remember, if you still dream

and still interact with your emotions your pineal gland is very much alive. It is only dormant in some areas and has atrophied to some degree because of abuse and lack of use.

Research reveals that fluoride is the number one reason for this disaster in our modern day. Along with mercury, pesticides, processed foods, synthetic calcium, artificial sweeteners, air fresheners and synthetic fragrances, alcohol, toothpaste, cigarettes, processed beverages, and MSG. Also, any flavor enhancers, food coloring, additives, binders, preservatives, fillers and this is not a complete list.

Besides stopping these items from entering your body, you must work on eliminating the toxins that already contaminate you. They are stored in all parts of your body, and the project will be a major one. Here are a few things you can do but, in addition, research the Internet for ways to purify and rebuild your body.

Some steps you can take are to add these to your diet: Supplementing with MSM, activator X, boron, melatonin, iodine, raw cacao, citric acid, garlic, distilled water and apple cider vinegar. You can also use Teas of passionflower, and St. John's Wort, but limit your intake to four cups daily. Melatonin 1mg only at night. It is the left brain that keeps you awake because it will not shut-up, and melatonin will solve this problem by giving your left brain a tranquilizer.

I was told that this exercise has been passed down through the centuries from the Tibetan monks. They used it to achieve oneness through trance meditation. The purpose is to resonate your tone or sound to get in contact with yourself by calling your name.

I cannot be responsible for your success, so try it at your own risk. If you are ready to explore the higher realms of consciousness beyond the normal five senses, then this will help you.

It goes alone with the same concept as, "Singing in the Brain" that all magic starts with sound. In the beginning was the word, and the word was with God, and the Word was God, the same was in the beginning with God". KJV

Start with finding your comfortable TONE. Hum the musical scale until you find your comfort zone. It should be something within speaking range. You will know when you are comfortable with the sound you are creating.

Then practice saying your name at that tone, until you can harmonize every letter of your name. Your name is the name of your God, and it is very important for you alone. While doing this, you vary your volume and tone as if you were singing your name.

Sit in a comfortable position with your back straight and eyes closed. Now relax and mentally scan your body for any signs of tension. Take three deep breaths through the nose and exhale through the mouth taking all your tensions with breaths. While doing this visualize your pineal gland as your third eye and see it open to a loving universe where the only existence is total happiness.

Take another breath again through the nose and this time hold it. Before you exhale, pucker your lips and place your tongue between your teeth. Press your teeth gently down on your tongue as you slowly exhale through your puckered lips. Now, do that again while saying or humming your name until all the air is expelled from your lungs. By humming a musical variation, this puts your effort into the right brain functions.

Repeat this exercise a total of three times then wait 24 hours and do it again. Do this for three days, then skip a day, then three days, then skip a day, then three days. A total of three squared, = 9 times. You can repeat this cycle in thirty days if you wish, but you should feel the effect of it in combination with your routines of Meditation, Visualization, and Self-Hypnosis.

Another source of reclaiming yourself is to get away from electromagnetic pollution in your environment. Take a walk-through nature; enjoy Mother Earth and Father Sun.

CHAPTER TEN

VISUALIZATION

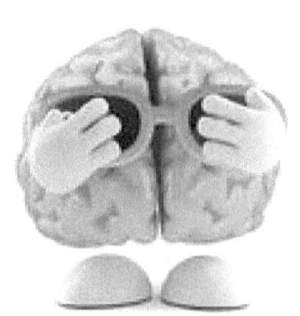

You grew up knowing that your mother had an eye in the back of her head. Regardless of what you did, she knew, especially if it was something you were not suppose to do. As a child, you knew that eye existed because mom proved it daily. Now as an adult have you ever questioned its existence? Or wondered what that was all about and if you also might have an eye in the back or your head?

Was it called mothers intuition, an extra sense or could she actually see you? The answer to all the questions is, 'Yes'. Mothers have an invisible knowing when it comes to their offspring. Knowing is a sense of seeing with the mind's eye.

Visualization means seeing an image without the use of your two physical eyes. You see it inside your head with the third eye. You can call it seeing with a small TV in your head or seeing on the back or your eyelids. It is accomplished with your eyes closed, so you are not using your normal vision. In this way, you can use your imagination or your intuition to "see." This is called imagery, which is a spontaneous subconscious reaction of feeling or thought. To create something in the mind's eye as a deliberate action is called visualization.

Visualization and imagery are often considered to be two totally different modalities. To keep things simple, I have concluded they are the same. When you visualize, you are forcing your mind to use the pineal gland. Visualization exercises are number one in directing focused energy into the third eye to activate the process of seeing and not just looking. Your creative imagination visualizes a thing, and then the energy of your mind brings it to life. It creates a magnetic field around your pineal gland provoking it to produce DMT, a hallucinogenic drug that can give you a sense of euphoria. It also gives you use of your imagination and the ability to Visualize. The more you force your pineal gland to work the more energy flows through your body.

Visualization has many schools of thought along with titles and conditions giving it a regimented behavior. The question at hand is what came first, Visualization or the pineal gland? I say the pineal gland because nature gives you the tool before it lets you use it. So, I am in hopes you read the chapter on the pineal gland already so you can better understand visualization.

Basically, there are three types of visualization; Receptive, programmed, and guided. Receptive it comes to you, programmed you go get it, and guided another person is involved and leads you through a programmed scene.

First you can visualize with your eyes open in the form of daydreaming or you can close your eyes and use your mind's eye as in nighttime dreaming. You use your inner vision whenever you dream or daydream. By consciously controlling this image, you can take another step and constructively create a visual concept. It is then a Right Brain business, as it becomes a higher intellectual level on the ladder of your mind and the chakras. Visualizations should collect data that can transform from invisible to visible. The crown chakra reaches into its vortex until it touches the pineal gland where Prana, or god's energy flows to the center of the head. When you meditate and visualize, energy is ascending the kundalini. The energy flows up and down like the angels on Jacobs ladder.

When you read a book, the author paints a picture for you in the form of words. Your brain puts those words in an understandable design for you. You absorb the meaning, visualize the picture and identify with the character. However, you approach the information you rescued from the book; you required visualization to store it as a memory.

When you first start a serious meditation practice, you will start getting flashes of intuition, and strange ideas that cause you to wonder about its source. It helps when using visualization to create a mood. Calm and relaxation are the zones you aim for, and it goes hand and hand with meditation. Although there is a strong link with meditation, it does not always accompany visualization.

In programmed visualization, you shut your eyes to see with your single minds eye and not your physical two eyes. Note when you do this how little you perceive about what your eyes see. Try this exercise: Shut your eyes and stand at your front door as if you were a stranger. Then knock or ring the doorbell. Exactly what does your door look like, and do you have a bell that chimes? The door opens and what do you see, did you leave it a mess or is it nice and tidy. See what is hanging on the walls or sitting on the shelves. Now see if you see anything unusual, something you do not remember having. You might be in the future seeing something you are planning to obtain. Later check to see if you were correct in what you saw.

Often when doing reading for someone I use this technique to visit their environment to answer questions for them. Like I lost something and need to find it, or I want a new vehicle, what do you see in my garage next month?

Using this same technique close your eyes and see yourself getting that job or a raise in pay, winning that special game, or passing that test. Scientific research shows that winning in competition has a direct connection with subconscious levels of our mind and visualization of success. Research also shows the same type of success with the use of hypnotherapy that is a more intense form of visualization.

The most popular style is guided imagery. It is where you follow the words of a narrator and go to peaceful places to receive pleasant rewards. With knowledge of self-hypnosis and access to the subconscious, you can take yourself on an enjoyable trip in the now or in past life regression. If you choose you can even travel into the future because there is no such thing as time, there is just now.

In Hypnotherapy, Guided Visualization is the method usually applied; it settles the mind and gives you a great feeling that the entire scene is real. And once you claim the reality of the scene it becomes a fact.

By just stepping aside and viewing as an observer, you can watch an entire movie in your head. It would be receptive visualization, and although you are in complete control, it is in the form of a director. You often revisit your memories like this, and as you view the script that your memory gives you, adjust the parts of the scene that makes healing possible. I call this the 'What if zone'. Just don't let it beat you with guilt.

Many successful people credit their success with creative visualization. That is using your mind to create the image by seeing yourself doing something or being somewhere. Success has to start with the dream or idea, which is part of that vision, and then following it with action. Everything exists in the imaginary world before it becomes reality. When you focus your vision on your talent, the product becomes easier to produce.

For most of my life, I designed and produced unique, unusual new age jewelry, and most of my items were totally detailed in the chambers of my head with my eyes closed. I created every design detail in every way it could be done and worked out the details and corrected the defects in my head before I carved it in wax. I saved myself time and disappointment because, if it could not work in imagination, it would not work in physical form. While working on the imaginary image I often found myself moving my physical hands because although there was nothing in my hands, I could feel the shape of the image in my head.

Einstein was the master at mastering his imagination, and here are a couple of his quotes. "Your imagination is your preview of life's coming attractions, and imagination is more important than knowledge. Logic will get you from A to B Imagination will take you everywhere. The true sign of intelligence is not knowledge but imagination."

"These thoughts did not come in any verbal formulation. I rarely think in words at all. A thought comes, and I may try to express it in words afterward."

Try this as a practice exercise. We all get mail now before you pick up your mail, do not guess at what it contains. Take a moment to slow your mind then take a couple deep breaths and shut your eyes. See yourself going to the mailbox, pause in front of it put the key into the lock then turn and open. Take the mail out piece by piece, analyzing the content of your mail. Now go get your mail and see how close you were to seeing your mail before you received it.

Here is another one, your telephone rings and do not look at caller ID instead shut your eyes and see who is ringing your bell. After you practice this one for a while, you will see the face before the phone rings, or you will walk to the phone and dial them as they are dialing you.

You will be surprised at what you see with your third eye, you can watch others walk around your environment as if your third eye was a surveillance camera. You can mentally tune in on any area you have the right to be.

Close your eyes and see you getting that job or a raise in pay, winning that special game, or passing that test. Scientific research shows that winning in competition has a direct connection with subconscious levels of our mind and visualization of success. Research also shows the same type of success with the use of hypnotherapy that is a more intense form of visualization. Medical institutions are fast being aware of the usefulness of both visualization and hypnosis as a form of rehabilitation.

Dreaming and Astral travel
When you go to bed, focus your attention on the third eye and visualize the image of your perfect night's sleep. Or ask for the answer to that day's unsolved problem and you will activate the third eye and solve your dilemma. That is probably where we got the statement just sleep on it.

Any form of sight inside the head is a form of visualization whether it is voluntary or involuntary. Dreams and Astral Travel are the two common forms of involuntary visualization. Astral travel is a dream in HD. It is like having an out of body experience, which can often become a teleportation.

I can only explain astral travel, as I know it from personal experience. During dream sleep when the brain is at a determined frequency, the door opens, and I fly out. I fly like a bird and have all the sensations of moving through space. I land and take off with no problems. I go to any destination I choose, by just thinking of myself there. Often, I go to research the topic of the day, but in my younger years I would sometimes get into trouble because I have disturbed some of my friends by visiting them in the night. They claim to have seen me standing in the room. When confronted with these appearances, I could often tell them the exact time and place.

While flying around I liked to 'show off' to any people that were watching, and I usually drew a crowd. I would then put on an acrobatic presentation followed by an instruction session on how they could also fly.

Just before you fall asleep, you can visualize taking an astral trip that night and after a habitual effort it will happen. The first time this occurs; it will probably wake you up, in fright, and you will crash back sometimes giving yourself a headache. Just keep visualizing and you can learn how to be a pilot.

Now let's look at what a dream actually is, and show you how to turn your dreams into therapy. Dreams are forms of venting and structuring your daily living. If you can learn to remember and analyze your dreams, you will have a window into the inner working of your life through your subconscious mind.

There are no experts on dream interpretations, only therapists that utilize your dreams to support other symptoms you are exhibiting in the course of your clinical visit. Do not let someone tell you what your dream means; it is your dream, ask yourself what it means. A therapist can suggest hypothetical solutions, but you must put your puzzle together. An image could represent different translations to different people in corresponding walks of life.

There are books on how to interpret dreams symbols, but I do not advise them and neither do I advise going for a past life regression when the therapist tells you what your past life's were. In both cases, you must see it yourself for it to be your truth. When you see yourself in a past life, it is hypothetically you and is being shown to you to assist your growth in this incarnation. Let's face it, how many Cleopatra's can there be in this time zone? By looking at it with a different perspective, how many lessons of Cleopatra can there be in our time you can understand how reincarnation translates.

Do not dismiss your dream as being unimportant just because you do not understand what it means. They are often in the language of symbols, and perhaps you have to learn that language to look at your dreams. A thought has no language; your mind translates your thought into words and stores in your left-brain. While your vision, either inner or optical, will do the same with an image but it will store that information in the right-brain.

Have you ever awakened from a dream and found that you cannot move because you are paralyzed? Here is a little information that is not well advertised. Your brain puts your body is a state of paralysis while you slept to protect you from yourself. It is called the Tonic Motor Inhibition in which voluntary movement is impossible. There are times in your dreams you get angry with someone and whip the poop out of them. When you wake, you have not moved because if you had your bedmate, thet would have taken a beating while dreamed. You can get frightened in your sleep, and you cannot run fast enough, your heart races but your body can't move.

Rapid Eye Movement activity is referred to as REM Movement happens when you are dreaming. It has no time limit and can often last several hours. Your sleep activity is in four stages that can be measured by the length of your brain waves. Each is lasting about one hour and runs consecutively. You repeat these as cycles several times each night. Your dreams sometimes change scenes for each cycle.

Lack of sleep is unhealthy, and no sleep can kill you. All day you are exposed to the appetite of your senses. And your brain is obligated to document all the data it can acquire. You may not see and hear all the details of the image before you, but your inner sight does, and every detail is filed, for future use. You have unlimited internal storage, but your short-term hard drive will usually handle about 14 hours of data collection before it is ready to crash. You fall asleep so your brain can download and file all the data you collected. It deletes some of it, files some of it and reacts to some of it in the form of dreams. So train yourself to be aware then relax, let go and let the melatonin do its job.

Altered memory visualization is used, in resolving past

conflicts and calming anger. When you watch your memory recreate an image, you can release the negative parts of the memory and introduce a calm, peaceful, forgiving memory. With a little practice, you can easily reduce the negative feelings and replace it with positive emotions.

To visualize is to think in a photo form. The eye was the instrument of thought, and the artist's ability to make pictures provided a special medium in which to carry out "thought experiments". This view, however, has been supplanted by the development of quantum mechanics and other abstract disciplines in which the objects of thought are all but impossible to visualize. The manipulation of abstract representations— if it occurs—does indeed seem to be a mode of thinking that is not visual.

CHAPTER ELEVEN
MEMORY

Memory is all around us and exists in all forms of nature in present past and future. You are no exception, being part of nature you must respond in a natural way. Your greatest asset is you can consciously change your memories instead of relying entirely on the process of evolution. The physical structure of your brain is modified each time you add a new memory, as it constantly upgrades itself. Regardless of what you think, you will never run out of the needed space to occupy the billions of memories you wish to store there.

Today's Internet market exposes us to sophisticated electronic advancements in computers, cell phones and more, which are totally mind-boggling. However as sophisticated as they might be, they cannot compete with the hidden abilities you house in your head.

We play brain games that are supposed to improve selected aspects of our memory along with the quality of our old age years. These benefits are small in comparison to the benefits gained by focusing on a proper diet. Your memory good or bad depends totally on how you trained, programed, exercised, and use it. Remember the old saying, " If you don't use it, you lose it." Science classifies the brain as a muscle, so to get the most out of any muscle, exercise is necessary.

Your memory is modified every time you input information through your five senses, as well as the numerous senses you may not even realize you have. This new information shuffles itself into existing memories to form a revised library of current information available for recall.

You have three basic types of memory; short-term memory, long-term memory, and recall memory. Rapid information loss occurs almost at once in the short-term memory because you can only remember an average of about seven things at any given time. Without a method of consciously converting short time items into long-term memories, you quickly lose the items. As fast as you access new things, the short-term library rolls over, and you lose the items. They seem to go to the same place your last night's dreams went. You know you had them, but they got away before they were imprinted.

Then there is the recall memory that is your search button, and it is always looking for something and often gets its files confused. When this happens your memory does not always recall situations as they were, it often fills in details that may or may not have existed at the time the memory was formed. Or it might have recalled opinions of others as if they were your memories. Your memories are your personal library and contain numerous updates, and you can trick yourself into thinking all your memories are facts and that they are all your memories. Fact or not they belong to you, even if you borrowed them from someone else, and you are entitled to keep them. You have the license to do with them as you choose. They exist entirely in your head as part of your brain and these cells often play tricks on you just to make you happy. Your imagination can create a detailed situation and place it in your long-term memory. Later, you may recall this as a real image instead of an imaginary one because your brain only collects data; it does not file as 'fact' or 'fiction'. The court of law does not respect recall memory as being fact.

Last, you have a long-term memory that is more powerful and impressive than any computer on today's market. It has limitless storage with an almost instant recall. Adding memories does not mean you must forget something to gain space for new updates, always remember you have unlimited recourse. The more you use, the more you have, making memory limitless.

The most difficult things to remember are numbers, the next names, and you probably thought that is just you. Well to your surprise that is everyone. There is a solution to this dilemma if you consciously create a system of recalling numbers and names utilizing some form of imagery. That transfers the short-term memory to long-term memory so you can retain it forever. Example, you just met 'Donald Stanley,' your mind can paint an instant photo of Donald Duck standing on one leg with a box of Stanley tools. You will never forget his name because you will instantly recall the photo and then remember the name.

The brain consists of two characteristics, visible and invisible. The visible brain is a physical 3lb glob of fat and water that can be scientifically dissected and studied to reveal detailed facts about its form. This study tells nothing about its function because that belongs to the invisible brain. That is much more complicated and requires special equipment to analyze its capabilities or capacities. Thinking and memory fall into this invisible world. Although the philosophy of how and why it works has and is currently being analyzed, it's studying goes back to BCE. It was Pythagoras Plato, Socrates, and others, who first analyzed and formed opinions based on their belief. Since there has never been a way to detail the facts about this magic, it exists in the category of theory. The mind, thinking and memory are still in the classification of metaphysics, where there are thousands of opinions but not much solid evidence.

Evolutionary psychologists have done studies on how memory does or doesn't work. These are usually a singular study for which they write a paper that gets published and then becomes part of a textbook saying now on this date it is a fact. Only in the past century and mostly the past 30 years has research expose dependable results.

Researchers claim your image memories are your most fantastic memory recall department. They say you can recall an image with more clarity and detail than the information deposited by other senses. They seem to overlook the facts of how your primitive brain developed and functions through the pineal gland.

Your memory has a special way of relating the shape and colors of nature to the prenatal survival instincts and uses basic geometric forms to create the photos that imprint long-term memory. Without memory, you could exist but have no point of reference for the things that motivated your daily activities. It is your memories that help you understand yourself as they link you to your future.

All research has an impact on collective learning, and I am a firm believer that if you want something done correctly you must do it for yourself. I have found that you will listen to yourself before you listen to others. You will take your personal advice before you take the advice of others. That by talking to yourself you solve your problems when others cannot solve them for you. If you tell yourself something, you will remember it longer than if someone else tells you. My conclusion is the way to improve your memory is to include your friends, namely me, myself and I into your conversation. You are your best teacher, and all traditional belief structures say, 'Look within to find yourself.' Programming your memory by talking to yourself; remember that you alone know the true sound of your voice. You hear the exact frequency of your voice, from inside your head. That frequency is important to your personal sanity because it controls your brainwave patterns. Outsiders can brainwash you only if they understand and utilize this reality and know your frequency.

To forget is the absence of memory. Where did the information go if it was once a memory? It is logical to state: 'If you improve your ability, not to forget you likewise improve your ability to remember.' Forgetting is the failure of the memory to remember. If we reduce forgetting, we increase memory. There are brain games that you can practice accomplishing this and help strengthen brain functions, both visible and invisible. Meditation and Visualization are the most powerful and require only self to accomplish.

Let's look at an interesting study that concluded, although hypnosis will drastically impact and improve almost any aspect of your daily life, there have been no studies that show it has any effect on your memory. So let's not judge hypnosis on studies that have not happened. Let's practice self-hypnosis and do our own studies. Personally, I have found that outside improving the methods I apply to remembering I credit self-hypnosis with the longevity of post-hypnotic suggestions.

Also, consider implicit memory. It is a type of memory in which previous experiences aid the performance of a task of recall without you having the conscious awareness that these previous experiences existed. Example, you just travel to a new place only to find you remember being there before. But you cannot remember when you were there or other details. You only remember the place in its exact detail. You have trace memories, and if you worked on it long enough, you could probably put the puzzle back together. That can explain the difference between remembering an experience or remembering the image.
The more you know, the more you can remember and the more you can recall. So, to be the life of a party, just keep learning.

CHAPTER TWELVE

THEORY OF MIND

Because mental states are not observable, all information about the mind must be a 'Theory'. The professional world has many definitions for the term, 'Theory of Mind', going all the way back to Sigmund Freud, 'the Father of Psychoanalysis'. The modern definitions refer to the growth and learning skills of children. They relate the term to the ability of the child that has started to realize that his small world is influenced by his environment and that others may have differing opinions and ideas from his. Their theory involves the child's ability to recognize other feelings and emotions and can respond to them as well as himself, with the respect that others who might not always share their views.

Subconscious programming starts at birth. At birth, you have a primitive mind, embedded with the animal instinct known as 'fright and flight.' You know love and comfort and fear heights and loud noises. From that point, you form associations and identification. You are exposed to unknowns, that when identified and converted into known, are magically posted on your memory board. It is here that you learn good equals positive, and bad is negative, which translates into rewards and punishment. Your conscious mind is developing, and you are forming a conscience.

These memories are your life script and contain everything you have learned. For most of us, we were about eight before we understood logic and reason. That being the critical age for the development of the basic rules of conscious thinking. Only 12% of your mind is your learning area utilizing three major players: identification, association, and response. From here you become the author of your life story.

This memory board is your subconscious mind, containing your 'knowns' and your 'unknowns', and it is always more comfortable with the things you know than it is with the unknowns. The unknowns sometimes become the things you fear until you can change them from, unknowns to known. It is what mind control is all about, giving your conscious mind the ability to read your memory board and change it if you wish. You then re-remember it, as you want it to be, not always as it was.

It is important that you realize own your mind. No one can enter it without your permission. You do not have to share it with anyone unless you choose to do so. Know you can change your mind at any time you choose, and that means you can even reprogram old memories and remember them as new ones. The toolbox you need for this job is Meditation, Visualization with Imagery and Self-hypnotherapy.

How often do you have to think about remembering something you know that you know, but something hides that memory file from you? Visualization is your friend, here you can tell the file clerk to retrieve the file by time, date or subject matter.

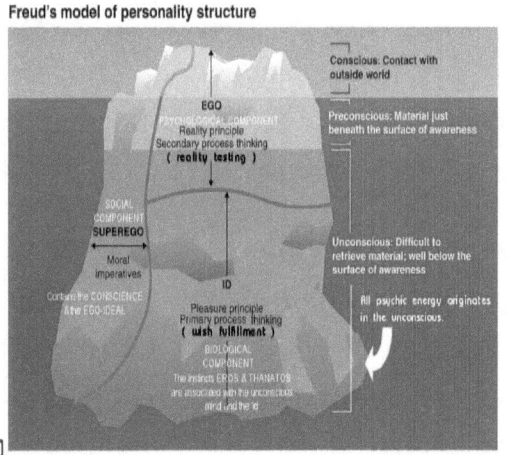

Freud theorized a structural model of his theory of the mind as an iceberg floating in the water. He believed that the driving force of life included our emotions and in; with our interaction with life. He perceived that some of the life experiences were unavailable to us at a conscious level. So he pictured the mind as an iceberg floating in the sea of primordial matter. His iceberg was divided into three sections, the upper section being the 'conscious' mind. It was that part of the mind that we are aware of, and it protrudes 12% above the waterline. The lower section, being the 'sub-conscious' mind occupied the balance of 88% of your mind. Below the water so out of sight, out of mind. Then he inserted an overlapping central area between these two, which he labeled the 'preconscious' mind.

This belt has also been called the 'critical mind', which is the term I favor. It is that diaphragm between the conscious and sub-conscious minds and spans an undetermined % of shared space. It forms the belt between the major players in your head, acting as a neutral area where you can negotiate with yourself. Freud never states how wide this overlapping belt could be, or what % of which mind it enveloped. So I take the liberty to label this seem as sharing 2% of the conscious mind and 8% of the sub-conscious mind and seeing it as a belt called 'critical' mind. I am suggesting that the critical mind is your editorial department, as you retrieve a memory from your memory board in your sub-conscious library. You pause this memory in the critical mind to review that memory while the conscious mind sits in judgment as to the accuracy of its details. If details prove to match, in reality, or in your today's conscious opinion, the recall is granted.

You must consciously establish an entrance through this barrier to gain free flowing information between conscious and subconscious minds. You create this doorway with the use of meditation, visualization, or self-hypnosis. Once you have consciously gained access through this doorway, you can, at any time, reprogram your thoughts, actions, reactions, and memories.

Your perceived thoughts and present actions live in the

conscious mind while your memories reside in the subconscious mind. We are continuously creating conscious thinking while parking these thoughts in the memory department. Most of us never realize that these thoughts and likewise memories are subject to editing and updating by the judgement of your mind that wears the title of your conscience.

The Critical Mind is that important player in successful singing to yourself, to gain whatever you want. You can envision it as a doorway that gains access to your subconscious mind, where all the memories that make you a total person are neatly filed. You should naturally have a free-flowing access to this energy and information in both directions from conscious to subconscious, but you do not. You have to visualize the doorway through this area to penetrate into your inner minds. Nothing is easy, but nothing ventured, nothing gained. So start practicing.

Retrieve any memory and change the details then remember it as a corrected memory. Reprogram the incident already programmed in your memory library. Example: I just gotta have another cigarette.' Retrieve that memory then reprogram it as 'I used to smoke cigarettes but now, I can't stand the thought of them.' ' Or, I am fat because it is genetic.' Reprogram the memory; I am overweight because of bad eating habits that I intend to correct.' Success is a matter of how we approach our library of self.

Freud's story continues: He concluded that our minds were constantly in conflict, which creates anxiety and discontent while generating physical and psychological traumas in our body. These seemingly unbalanced symptoms of memory congregate in our critical mind and barricade the proper avenues of traffic from conscious to subconscious minds. It was Freud's conclusion that by using hypnotherapy the critical mind could be neutralized granting passage of the greater part of yourself, namely your conscious and sub-conscious minds.

Freud theorized three divisions of the mind and named them the id, the ego, and superego. Human consciousness is altered by the fundamental animation of thought in the realm of the sub-consciousness, stimulating the productivity of the body. Once again, challenging the true meaning of Rene Descartes's quote, "I think, therefore I am."

Fraud concluded: The ID Is a set of instinctual traits related to the most primitive animated physical activities that occur at the seat of Consciousness. That physical emotion is controlled by the pleasure principle, which demands satisfaction with no regard to consequence. It is your true animalistic nature depriving conscience of moral right and wrong. It is controlled, by the fright/flight factor, which is connected to the autonomic nervous system and generated through our animal survival instincts.

Then comes the understanding of gratification, which

opens the reality principle and introduces 'Eros', [drive] to the ego. Born of ID, EGO will forever remain its servant and through suggestion and experience will perfect the art of quantum jumping between me myself and I, with Logic and reason as its building blocks.

The super-ego creates the frustrations in the mind between your conscience and your idealism by programming you with guilt and fear, prejudice, and doubt. Your inborn ID demands respect to its self-pride, in opposition to learning goals and ambitions instilled by society.

In summary, Subconscious is 88% of the mind below the level of our awareness. It is that part of the mind, responsible for the reflexive responses of natural animation. It is the id motor responses, contains the positive and negative associations we make throughout our life.

The Conscious mind is the 12% of the mind that we are most aware of because we relate to logic, reasoning, and decision-making along with willpower. When you speak your mind, it is the conscious mind doing the talking and the one you are referencing.

The Critical Mind is the gray area of the mind that sits between conscious and sub-conscious and is part of both. The critical mind utilizes conscience, that is the active part of the conscious mind, as a filtering system between conscious and sub-conscious mind. The Subconscious mind does not understand the word 'consequence' or have a conscience; it only does what the conscious mind commands of it.

Theory of the mind divides the mind into four stages or areas that are: the primitive area, given to you at birth and containing the fright/flight response. Being directly related to your animal nature it is affected by loud noises and by falling. The Conscious area formed when you were about 8 or 9, which introduced logic and reason into the decision making of the mind. The Critical area formed at the age of 10 which filtered message units into accept or reject and developed your opinions. Next is the Modern Memory area that handles the 'Known,' those memories that are common to you, the ones that you know as facts in your life.

Although today's world of psychology declares that, Freud's interpretation of the mind is archaic, their reestablished definition of the mind follows the same fundamental principles. Freud also utilized hypnosis as part of his psychological practice. The fields of imagery, as well as hypnotherapy, were not recognized as a division of the medical profession at that time, but things are changing at a rapid rate. Freud was a pioneering groundbreaker and so-called father of all psychiatry, but he also endorsed hypnotherapy and visualization.

Today's scientists and mathematical experts claim that the mind is a supercomputer making it easy to hack into and change. They credit this ability as belonging only to self, and if you can learn how to reprogram your mind, you can drastically increase your intelligence.

Jeri Lee C.Ht.

Echoes

Have you heard them?
Sounds from afar
Are they whispers from
Your past?
Holograms of illusions
Or part of a dream?
Are they vibrations of music
From a cosmic choir?
Or lessons of life
In a reincarnated form?
Just out of reach
Of exact knowing.
Are they just a
Tantalizing frustration?
Their format is
For those who are aware
Listen closely and
You will know
The truths that
Make you – YOU

CHAPTER THIRTEEN

CONSCIOUSNESS

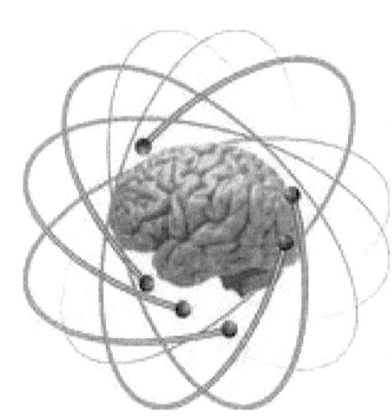

Our ancient history that survived Constantine and the dark ages shows that the mind and consciousness was always a curiosity. It has been studied science as far back as Socrates, Plato, and Aristotle. This subject matter and possibilities have, been theorized, by most of the distinguished minds that blanketed the halls of fame and gained recognition through such prizes as the Nobel Peace Prize.

Most students of this science considered the mind and mental disorders as being of supernatural origin. Some of our most prestigious organizations have designated rituals, designed to remove the bad thoughts and reprimand the demons that overpower the mind of their victims. I have witnessed several such demonstrations and can personally state that the executor should be the executed. As far back as the 4th century; Hippocrates [a Greek physician] determined that mental disorders had to be a physical problem and had nothing to do with the world of beliefs or superstitions. History shows there are many schools of thought on every theory in every generation but because of the invisibility of the mind it cannot by isolated in a Petri dish and thus can not be scientifically proven.

A look at history shows that Freud established a criteria on the mind and matter that modern psychologist mimic with new names. Freud, along with most of his peers through history, have given many names to the same mind function. To avoid a religious coloration, some chose to neutralize the sanctity of the super conscious mind to minimize the authenticity of a God.

I include Freud's interpretation as reference material, as I dissect the mind in a little different way but include most of Fraud's theories.

First, Freud and most students and professors in this field all agree that we have a conscious mind. Fraud gives it this definition: Your conscious mind includes everything that you are aware of, it is the source of your mental processing enabling you to think and talk rationally. It contains your memory and the ability to retrieve the memory that is not part of the conscious mind.

Freud then addresses the second mind as the preconscious mind and labels it the home of ordinary memory. He states that even though we are not consciously aware of it, our memories are all stored there, and we can retrieve them, at any time by the conscious mind.

Carl Jung said that there were limits to what we can hold in our conscious focal awareness. So an alternative area of one's knowledge and prior existence is necessary, and he agreed with Freud in that the assigned area must be the preconscious mind.

The third mind he labeled the unconscious mind and gave it the responsibility of controlling our feelings, thoughts, urges and a special class of memories that were outside of our conscious awareness. Freud put all our unacceptable or unpleasant emotions is this mind including pain, anxiety or conflict. Most importantly he recognized that this mind continues to influence our behavior and experiences even though we have no awareness of its underlying influences.

The procedure I am introducing you to in this book involves the utilization of your conscious mind and using the way it can control your subconscious mind, which in turn influences the behavior of every cell in your body. If you understand what the mind is, you can better control the function of all its parts, related to and under the direct supervision of your conscious control.

Physics and metaphysics have always been at odds as to the definitions, relationships, and functions of all the forms of consciousness. Based on my lifelong research in the study of metaphysics, I take a metaphysical approach.

We are going to take a courageous look at my version of the mind or minds. Most studies of the mind involve mental institutions and the study of psychoanalysis. However being crazy is not the only criteria for the need to understand the mind. I find that today's psychologists, along with most doctors, are not in the business of finding answers to your problem. Instead, they research what pill will best cover up the symptom instead of finding the cause. My son is a candidate for this club of expensive "Happy pills," and their companion "don't give a shit" pills. On days that he gets his meds mixed up, he says, " he is not happy but doesn't give a shit about it." Mental disorders are physical diseases and belong to the physical brain not the consciousness of the mind.

In my opinion, there are four categories of mind, each having their unique function:

Consciousness: as a Noun it means the state of being awake and aware of one's surroundings, to be mindful, having conscious knowledge of something.

Sub-conscious: it is on the edge of consciousness and invisibly controls all your body functions while it harnesses and files your personal data and packages it as memories.

Higher consciousness is transcendental reality or your god-self. This is the part that connects you with your Creator and has a memory of the Source.

Unconscious: is an area of vacuum that separate conscious mind from its contemporary stages, it is the prelude to death, which introduces the resurrection of life.

Understand that these four units make one product called the mind, which functions through a physical organ called a brain, which belongs to something called a body, which you claim is your personal self.

So, is the mind part of the physical or mental world, or is it located on an invisible spiritual plane? Is your mind proof of consciousness or is it consciousness itself? Is your mind your consciousness or is being conscious your mind? Then what is Sub-consciousness, does it mean less than or below consciousness? How does Super-consciousness fit into the pattern and what makes it 'super'? Is it your imagination that you even have something labeled your mind, or could it be a hologram of your parent's illusion?

These are all simple questions that baffle the most learned of the scientific world. The ancient scholars of philosophy pondered over the same questions our modern philosophical world is still theorizing. Proving that the jury is still out on solving the mystery of life, but, needless to say, there are many books claiming facts on the subject.

Most people are fully aware of their conscious mind, which includes their day-by-day behavior and their belief structure. However, at the same time they are totally unaware of their subconscious mind and the part it plays in their existence. They would be surprised to know that the subconscious mind is over a million times more powerful than the conscious mind they call self. Then, to realize that their unknown subconscious mind operates over 98% of our body functions, without even asking permission from their EGO.

Mr. EGO or our conscious mind, likes to believe it is in full control, but it is usually only aware of itself and its personal wants and wishes. Daily activities of living consume most of the activity displayed in this department. It operated by habit with little or no concern for creative activity.

The conscious mind often gets consciously confused with a conscience. Both words belong to mind control but have a uniquely different part to play. They are both part of EGO and conscious mind. Neither subconscious nor super-conscious mind has a conscience. The subconscious mind belongs to your Animal Nature with survival as its prime goal. Your super conscious mind is your god-self, and it does not need a conscience.

Let's get a better understanding of the forms of consciousness and state that conscious and unconscious belong together as the top and bottom of awareness. You have differing degrees of consciousness awareness relating to your interplay with vital brain waves. Based on your focal point you are always in one of these numerous levels, which I detail in the chapter on the brain. It has nothing to do with your subconscious or your super conscious mind. The reason being is that your conscious mind is your thinking mind and your subconscious, and super conscious minds do not think. But it's a fact, that each division of mind has a job and is totally efficient in its assumed occupation.

Your subconscious mind maintains homeostasis in your body without your conscious thought or knowledge. It is your accumulative library of personal life experiences housed as a collection of your thoughts and feelings. It is always on duty and never sleeps. It also never shuts up, and if you can learn to listen to it you can become wise. Since subconscious has no conscience, it cannot establish right from wrong, it likewise cannot think for itself.

When conscience, was introduced, to the conscious mind when evolution experienced a helping hand from the Gods. "Behold, the human is become as one of us, to know good and evil." Conscience is to be aware of right and wrong and the creation of morality and guilt in exchange for survival and natural instinct. The two words are both connected to mind behavior, the first being Awake the other being Aware.

Thinking is the gift of the conscious mind, which determines, by the choices it makes, the life and destiny of the body it utilizes. Thus, today you are the totality of all the choices you have made in your entire life. Are you happy with what you have produced?

Next in line is your subconscious mind, and the sub does

not mean less. It is more important to the existence of your living body that the sub-conscious mind functions in a proper order than for your conscious mind to think about it. The subconscious mind is in full control of that living blob of protoplasm you take for granted as your body. Its foremost responsibility is to control properly the invisible world of physics, which maintains all the natural functions of your anatomy. It is your personal Ph.D. in DNA.

Your conscious mind has a direct line of this Dr. Self with the authority invested in it from a super conscious mind to rework and repair its existing structure. So, you can think yourself, talk yourself, or even sing yourself healthy. Learn to take advantage of this natural unexposed gift.

Your subconscious mind is like a child on autopilot; it received your personal blueprint at birth. It implanted this knowledge into your brain with the do-it-yourself manual and a time capsule. Once that task was completed, that mind had the freedom to play, and for most cases has been on vacation. It automatically controls body functions; it tells the heart when to beat, the lungs when to take a breath, the kidneys how to collect fluid, the blood where to flow. It supervises all the natural body resources found in this blueprint. It cleverly camouflages the mysteries of life from the probing medical world because it was born with that wisdom implanted in its super conscious mind to successfully do that job.

The conscious mind often has a problem dealing with the

sub-conscious mind because it cannot get its attention. The subconscious mind listens to you all day while you are thinking, talking and doing things. It follows you around like a personal secretary, jotting down notes and parking them in memory files just in case you want to review them later. It is so preoccupied with its dedication to your natural needs it does not pay attention to your special wants. It just goes about its business and pretends no one lives in the Attic.

Your conscious mind must learn how to address the sub-conscious mind to get its attention. Meditation, visualization, and hypnotherapy are three of the best ways to earn respect of your sub-conscious mind.

The habits of your subconscious mind supersede all conscious control unless you deliberately take control of your conscious mind and do not just let it do its own thing. Once you are in the driver's seat, you can direct the subconscious mind to alter its course of programmed behavior to benefit your destiny.

Your subconscious mind thrives on the pleasures of the senses and tempts the conscious mind with an appetizing menu. The subconscious mind wants to keep the conscious mind happy: but remember, the sub-conscious mind has no conscience, so it glories in all the animalistic pleasures it can conceive.

As part of this trio; the subconscious mind is in the middle and thus becomes the mediator between your conscious mind and your super conscious mind. Your conscious mind cannot directly contact your super conscious mind; it needs the subconscious mind as the link to gain access.

Your conscious mind would fry itself if it attempted a direct connection to the super conscious. Think of your mind, as the total of me, myself and I. Me, being your conscious self, myself as your sub-conscious self, and I as your higher self. Then remember, "I am that I am, I am God/Goddess." Know that you are the total of the cosmos but also realize that there is no way you can conceive of your total potential.

The super-conscious mind is part of Cosmic Consciousness, and thus the inspiration of life itself. Your subconscious mind is your conscious messenger for cosmic communication. It is said, you cannot look at the face of God or survive in the direct presence of the creative energy. So, think of the super-conscious mind as radiation and the sub-conscious mind as the insulator. You can utilize the radiation but never come in contact with it.

It is also often referred to as the source, the library of knowledge where nature hides all things, present, past and future as one existence termed 'NOW'. Although this interpretation is often disputed by those supposedly, "in the know", many including myself, consider it a fact. In my first death experience I went there, I witnessed, I know.

When consciousness is unconscious does it still have a life? Modern medicine labels the subconscious mind as the unconscious mind, but my interpretation shows they have two distinctive behaviors. So I ask, what is the unconscious mind and how does it link itself with life? Seemingly, without life there is no mind, without a mind can there be life. Where is the 'Door of Death?'

When the brain has no life and is labeled brain dead, where is consciousness? Sub-conscious still exists because the body still functions carrying out the routine duties of the body. It has become unplugged from its source of conscious existence but is still very much alive expressing evidence of subconscious behavior.

There is a school of thought that links the soul with consciousness and designates proof by giving it a weight at the time of death. Several serious investigators of the phenomena have documented this theory. In the early 1900's Dr. Duncan MacDougall, a physician in Haverhill Massachusetts weighed patients at the moment of death and concluded that the soul weighed ¾ of an ounce. Then in 1988 Noetic Science carried out experiments on a larger group of patients at the time of death and updated the information to be 1/3 of an ounce. In the late 70's, second-hand information was that John Hopkins University was involved in research to validate this information and to prove the continuity of the conscious.

Many doctors have approached this study, and their conclusions are varied. But they all agree that the only possible explanation to account for the loss of weight is that there is a type of life force that leaves the body at the exact time of death. You may call it what you want, but most refer to it as the soul. Dr. Becker Mertens of Dresden stated in the German science publication 'Horizon' "that the logical conclusion is that the existence of the soul had been confirmed, and its approximate weight determined. Now, the challenge is to find the soul's exact composition; they said, "We are inclined to believe that it is a form of energy. But our attempts to identify this energy have been unsuccessful to date.

I must add that in my opinion; the soul is that individualized monad or spark of cosmic stuff that isolated itself into the substance that generated your consciousness. I am not sure what it weighs, but I am sure that it leaves the body at the time of death. And I am sure that it exits through the top of your head, and I am sure that it feels like a butterfly.

It was a beautiful spring day, and life was returning to my yard and the countryside around me. It was a great day to be alive, but my dear friend did not have that option; it was the day of her death. She was a professional student with two master's degrees, one of which was in botany, and Spring was her favorite season. So, there might be truth in the statement that we choose the time of birth as well as death. She taught me about the flowers in my yard, the ones to eat and what ones to leave alone. I did not take the time to learn enough from her, and now she was on her way to another existence. I watched for six months as that

C-monster sucked the life from her and today I was on my way to the hospital to say goodbye.

Her hospital room was humming with voices as a dozen friends carried on private conversations oblivious to the stench of death and the clinical reality that surrounded them. IMO, they lacked proper respect for the patient in the bed. Entering the room, I acknowledged none of them but went directly to the bedside of my friend and leaned over her, putting my right hand on her forehead and my left one on the top of her head. Putting my elbows on her pillow, I got close to her ear and started talking softly to her. I explained what was happening and what she should expect and released her from the physical. I gave her permission to leave. This conversation probably lasted 15 to 20 minutes. She was of course heavily drugged, in the grasp of the death rattle, which made her breathing noticeably loud. She started to relax as the breathing softened then she took a deep gasping breath and expired. At that exact moment, I was jolted into 'shock mode' for there was a cosmic butterfly that came out of the top of her head and escaped past my thumb and index finger and was gone. I realized I had been blessed for I had touched her soul. And I am sure that the soul is energy because I was on a HIGH for a week from the charge that butterfly gave me. The super conscious mind houses that butterfly soul and is part of Cosmic Conscious. It takes it through the door called death, which is an extension of life through reincarnation and rebirth.

The subject of mind and conscious cannot readily be discussed without involving the questions, "What is conscious?" and "What is its origin? It is important to realize that consciousness must always link itself to a form of intelligence.

We will always have a controversy between the theories that life can easily be explained in physicochemical terms without the metaphysical concept of a soul. It is my firm belief and one that I share with millions that Divine Consciousness being Universal Cosmos manifested everything from the energy of thought. That is not defining that energy as God or institutionalizing it with a religious concept. Everything in nature is part of that consciousness, and every part of nature has consciousness induced as a shared life essence.

Recent scientific experiments show that you can crush a rock to death. Minerals cannot be cohesive without a certain amount of consciousness attached to them. The chemical affinity of molecules that are needed to produce minerals are a form of consciousness. Every atom has a form of intelligence at its nucleus, thus has consciousness.

Consciousness is the evolution of life starting with the mineral kingdoms and graduating to the vegetable kingdom.

In the late 70's, I met Peter Tompkins and was introduced to his research with plants and enjoyed his book, "The Secret life of Plants." His research concluded that plant life has consciousness and that a head of lettuce screams when you attack it with a knife but does not mind being gently pulled apart by hands. He demonstrated collective consciousness, in that plants shared experiences and communicated.

He discovered that any environmental violence or negativity against nature disturbed his plants. They registered a reaction when a live lobster was dropped into a pot of boiling water or when eggs were cracked, for his breakfast omelet. They likewise responded to music and enjoyed classical but disliked rock music. His most impressive experiments showed that distance was not an equation in the response of his plants. They loved him and responded to his messages even if he was hundreds of miles away.

Science had established that life evolved from water, and Masaru Emoto has chronicled impressive research that focuses on consciousness in a drop of water. He exposed a drop of water to emotional experiences and then froze that emotion into an ice crystal that he then photographed. He collected water from global areas of interest and showed that geographic location impressed the crystal with uniquely different designs. His experiments included exposure to different types of music, and like Peter's plants, the water had a positive response to classical music and rebelled at rock and more so with hard rock. Dr. Emoto showed that water responded to isolated words and your mental intent that expressed that word. When you spoke of love or invoked cosmic blessings the ice crystal was perfectly formed. His photography proved that spiritual consciousness is positively magical. When you bless that which you partake of, regardless whether it is food, pleasure, or thought it is positively responsive to your life and how you live it. His most beautiful book is, the "Healing Powers of Water", and should be part of your collection.

The medical world has demonstrated that blood also holds memories and is affected by its donor, which makes you wonder about blood transfusions. In my life, I have had over a dozen units of blood introduced into my body and have often wondered if I was collecting foreign karma or if I was linking myself to unknown aspects of consciousness. Are the alien parts of my dreams, intended for someone else?

Yogi Maharishi Mahesh achieved fame as the guru of the Beatles, The Beach Boys, and many other celebrities; and promoted expanded thinking. He is credited with the proposal of the existence of a unique fourth state of consciousness based on physiology. His scientific studies delved into research of the physiological effects of Transcendental Meditation and the development of states of higher consciousness. He exposed those areas of consciousness previously relegated to mysticism.

His efforts showed how individual consciousness affects collective consciousness. He exposure the truth of this practice when in 1993 in Washington D.C. he gathered 4,000 like thinking meditating individuals with positive thought and dropped the crime rate by 15%. He proved like attracts like.

The question: Is consciousness the soul? I went out to the blog world, and the answers came in as 40% yes and 60% no and here are a few blog comments.

QUOTE "Our consciousness is what makes us distinctly us." "After death, sub-consciousness merges back into consciousness, which finally merges with the super consciousness."

QUOTE "I think what religious people define as the soul is another way to see consciousness, that thing that leaves when you die."

QUOTE "Without a soul a person would be an automaton reacting to reality without knowing. The source, physical features and location of the soul is not known. But the existence soul is obvious to people who have one."

QUOTE "Consciousness is like a multidimensional awareness of the All that is, the Big Picture; that is contained, in all forms of existence, in all creations on earth and beyond. Maybe consciousness and existence have a special affinity."

QUOTE "I do not think consciousness is your soul because I don't believe there is an extra thing inside us like the soul.

I think consciousness is just what it is, consciousness. There is no soul inside you that escapes when you die. You're alive because every part of your body is functioning properly."

QUOTE "Consciousness is not the soul. I believe when we die, our souls die with us."

QUOTE "I think that our souls are nothing more that neurological manifestations of our genetic programming and past experiences. I think that it is very hard for consciousness to die because consciousness is the universe. I think that even things that don't have minds [including plants and inanimate objects] have a conscience. I believe that we might truly die when the theoretical day comes that the universe collapses upon itself and is, destroyed."

QUOTE "I believe the Soul is a byproduct of brain function and there is no need to impose spirituality, to falsely comfort, yourself about living and dying, etc."

QUOTE "Yes consciousness is the soul, it is really more about how we think and what actions we make in reaction to the world."

QUOTE "Consciousness is a symptom of a soul, this knowledge you can understand by studying authorized Scripture, not by speculation."

QUOTE "Consciousness is not the soul; rather it is our

brain's memories in a modified state. Without consciousness we cannot live. It is the brain's memories of things taught and lived in a modified state while the soul is something that we are born with and grows with us."

QUOTE "Consciousness and the soul are two opposite things and you can have one without the other because you can have your soul while not being conscious. Therefore, concluding that those who are in a coma could have a soul, but meanwhile they do not have consciousness because they are in a comatose state."

QUOTE "Consciousness is not the soul and this is a question for Christians because it can be answered in many ways."

QUOTE "In my opinion there is no soul at all, you live you die, that's it."

This is an interesting cross section of beliefs and comments from the cyber world. It shows that we each have our personal thoughts on the subject with a wide range of opinions. Without a fact gauge, except nature and it's invisible shield, which opinions are closest to the 'real truth'?

I see Consciousness is all around me. The birds sing to me, and the sounds of the frogs and insect world lullaby me into dreamland. As a child, I learned to talk to the trees and communicate with nature while embracing the challenge of knowing what I instinctively knew. Then, I faced the opposition of what society and my environment wanted me to believe.

To conclude, know that if you can harness only a small portion of your conscious awareness, your mind would be the mustard seed that could move mountains. Knowing is based on Fact; belief, is based on Faith, which "F" do you follow?

CHAPTER FOURTEEN

SINGING - SOUND

Your thoughts are living things; they are images of quantum possibilities with endless creations. The sounds you utter are vibrations that manifest form in correspondence to those creative thoughts. You project an energy that is directed toward a target of known or unknown substance when you think. Your intention is the direction; your desire is the destination. The cause and effects are the generators that cultivate the growth of your projection. You are a creature of thought, as the extension of your body, the creature born of salt and water. Your thought was energized by the mind, transported at speeds that exceed light and travel to distances that transcend space. All this happens without you realizing that you just experienced a miracle.

A thought is a powerful substance, either individualized or collectively; it can promote action, generate energy and dissipate emotions. Behind every creation was a thought that expanded into a form. Like all things in nature, thoughts have a duality, a polarity of either positive or negative. They are magnetic as they gather together as clouds of energy fed by the attitudes of crowds of like thinkers. Thoughts become complicated when they create webs that blanket cultural cross-sections with planetary doubt. By mixing individual thoughts, you generate opinions that fuel combustibility. Combative thinking creates disagreements, battles and then wars. By now you should start to appreciate the power of a single thought. Grouped together they have strength in numbers. They can generate harmony or disharmony in humanity as well as other species. They can promote peace or conflict, according to the direction of the thought.

It is important to know that a thought is a frequency generated by the mind that travels at a speed faster than light. Thoughts can collect and disseminate data in the form of concepts as opposed to data in the form of the word. It's composition is that of ideas, as opposed to explanations and disseminates without discrimination to all that are capable of abstract thought.

Understand that the power of thought is important to the success of creating the self of your imagination. You must mentally create the product before you can harvest the fruit of success. You must think of yourself healthy before you can claim health.

This book flourished in the arena of sound; you can sing

yourself healthy with the vibrations produced by your mind. The thought is the most powerful unit of this collection, as it is the creator of the other elements, meditation, visualization, and self-hypnosis.

The harmonics of thought blended with sound is credited with the traditional concept of creation. In all cultures, all traditions, all ages, all religions, the unified question that supports their sameness is the search for the beginning and the fabrication of a creation myth. In this lesson, impress yourself with the knowing that if thought and sound can create, they can recreate and maintain. You can generate the image and discipline your cells to be obedient to this cause.

Sound takes the credit for the creation: "In the beginning was the word." [KJV John 1:1] It mattered not what the word was just that it was a sound. Then, "the Word was made flesh and dwelt among us." [KJV John 1:14]. The sound of a word, which is a vibration, a frequency, created form. The form is a physical solid called 'flesh' that was an active protoplasmic substance that could interact with its creator.

Sounds have special qualities; sound takes random particles and turns them into a form. The Word was a sound that turned matter and energy into a form, creating universal solidity with cosmic awareness. If a sound is responsible for the creation, it must also be capable of re-creation. That tells me that by using sound you can recreate the body you inherited at birth. The sound of your voice is your creative gift. With it you can re-create yourself and correct your health issues simply by talking or singing to yourself.

The resonance of sound creates everything; it is the frequency that surrounds us. The sound is the source of all energy, and when properly directed it focuses life consciousness into the 97% of our junk DNA permitting us to become "like unto God."

In Hinduism, the primordial creative source is the sound of OM. When sung or chanted it is on different frequencies, OM-MA-NI-PAD-ME-HUM.

The Egyptians sang us into creation with the six resident frequencies of the All-Seeing Eye of Horus. They make reference to the third eye called the pineal gland and designed the symbol of Horus in the shape of the brain honoring the importance of this gland.

We have the Christian Bible, and Jewish Torah, the Hindu Bhagavad Gita, the Chinese Buddhist Upanishads, the Muslim Quran and Vedas, and hundreds more. They were all inspired, by sound, to create symbols based on the frequency of sound vibratory patterns. The equilateral cross has four equal arms inside of the circle and was one of the first symbols to be classified, as a vibratory design, so was considered Holy. It is used by most ancient cultures including the Native American Indians, as their medicine wheel. Every frequency creates an individual sound pattern related to cosmic geometry. The ancient teachings state that God geometrized and creation transpired.

When you speak, you create a vibration that you interpret as sound because it has a frequency that can be measured. You have an ear, which is the specialized sensory organ that interprets that frequency into a sound wave that generates a noise. When you think you also send out a frequency that can be measured by instruments, although it is out of the sound level range for the ordinary person. There are some mammals, including some humans, that hear the frequency of the thought waves.

I am quite certain that the animals that live in my house know more about what I think than I do. Your pets understand more than you give them credit for, and the only thing that prevents them from speaking your language is the fact that they lack the proper set of, vocal chords. They express themselves in other forms of communication; unique to each species and often more sophisticated than we can understand. They create sounds that are characteristic of their identification and necessary for the survival of their species.

The human animal has a pair of vocal chords connected to a vibratory vocabulary sound that generate a mental pattern that is unique to our species. Every member of humans has a frequency that is as personal to their identity as their fingerprints and facial features. Like the snowflake that generates originality in every flake, humans perpetuates authenticity in every soul. Your vibrational frequency is uniquely your own and the exact sound of your voice is heard only by you.

I am sure that we have all heard our voice played back from a recording device. The first experience was unusually strange in that you did not recognize your voice. After exposure to this uniquely new sound, you learn to associate it with your personal identification. You cannot record the true frequency of your voice as you hear it, and likewise no one else can hear its true frequency. Your voice resonates within your skull and stays within your mind in the form of personal identity in the form of memory that you alone have the ability to utilize as part of the frequency of your body.

This frequency is your personal key and the secret to the success of your control over the function of your body, mind and soul. It opens the door to your inner self and resonates life through all the cells in your levels of existence. It induces a calming effect, over your collective consciences and becomes your own natural tranquilizer. Simply put, if you talk to yourself, the sound of your voice has a tranquil effect on you; it is your personal tranquilizer.

Nikola Tesla said, "The earth rings like a bell." He also stated that, by the redundancy of sound you could create a high-frequency vibration that would create energy. All the free energy you need out of the air. Tesla claimed, and sources are proving him correct that "Sound is the free fundamental energy on the planet and that sound waves travel beyond the speed of light".

Coral Castle is a popular tourist area in Hollywood, Florida. I first visited in the early 80s and have returned several times. I ceased to be amazed at how one extremely small man named Ed Leedskalnin could cut and move these giant coral boulders as he did. Not happy with where he first constructed his castle, he loaded his boulders onto his truck by himself and transported them to their present location. He would not expose his secret to anyone. In my research, I found a newspaper clipping stating that two young boys secretly watched him and said he lifted the rocks with an ice cream cone in each hand. In the Bible, the walls of Jericho came tumbling down because the trumpets blew. Compare the shape of the trumpet and the ice cream cone and ask, "Could he have been holding an instrument that produced a high frequency that enables gravity to be defeated?" Most ancient cultures have left evidence and stories of levitation with the mythology that states that large stones floated into place or that they were sung or hummed into place.

In the late 70's and early 80's, I was involved with a group that was experimenting with a mysterious black box and an intriguing idea called Radionics. We studied the works of Albert Abrams [1864-1924] and constructed our boxes with lots of dials that could be adjusted to various frequencies. We believe that diseases could be treated using radio waves or by generating prescribed frequencies. The United States FDA considered this practice pseudoscience, but today's scientific world has shown a renewed interest in modified versions of this practice. Many fields of alternative medicine are proving this theory as factual. In most cases, the black box has been eliminated from the practice.

A healthy body runs on energy and this energy functions at various frequencies. Each organ of this body has its personal frequency, and the combination of their frequencies produces an aura. If the body frequencies are out of balance, the body becomes ill. By energizing the body with the frequency needed the body, is brought into harmony, and proper health restored. Since all nonscientific concepts are theories, it is my theory that talking or singing to yourself creates a frequency, and this personal frequency contributes to the healing of your body.

We were also experimenting with water and sand and the designs they created when exposed to certain frequencies. The planet you walk on is 70% water, 30% land. The body you live in is likewise 70% water and 30% solid mass. Frequencies that affect your body can likewise affect planet earth; since it is a living organism that permits us to be parasitic, there must be compatible harmony.

As a frequency is applied to water or sand, it is mirrored by it geometric design. The lower frequency creates a simple design, and as the frequency elevates, the design becomes more complex. In viewing this phenomenon, you must realize the laws of nature are repetitive so if this applies to water and sand it also applies to you. When the sand or water resonates, it creates a sound similar to the sound you create when you think. Your thoughts and emotions are personal vibrations to which you and only you are exposed. They are held together by a vibratory pattern or frequency that resonates in harmony with the liquid crystal body in which you live.

When we think, we are sending out the sound because every frequency has a sound. Some are outside the range of human hearing. The sound then takes random particles and turns them into form, as "In the beginning was the word." That word was a sound that turned matter and energy into form, creating universal solidity with cosmic awareness.

Since every organ in our body vibrates at a certain frequency, when our thoughts, emotions and stresses, disrupt that frequency, and it is not harmonious to your various body parts, it creates illness. So in this way you create your own illnesses because you are what you think. You might have unknowingly created the illness that imprisons you at this time. However, you can knowingly undo what the unknown did. You can accomplish this by talking or singing to yourself, creating sounds and frequencies that resonate to your body harmony.

In the early 60s and 70s, metaphysical studies were not easily obtainable; there was no Internet, You-Tube or Wikipedia so you searched for a teacher and were fortunate if you found one. The saying 'When the student was ready the teacher was there' is a proven fact in my case. I was always ready, and the teachers were there.

We learn through fascination and appreciation, and both of these headings lead me to the work of the late Masaru Emoto. He researched the geometric patterns of water proving that water has memory and is more than a simple physical substance. It could show the emotional response with the interaction of thought, words, ideas, music, color, the environment, plants, or most objects. Water would respond either positively or negative to about anything he exposed to it. It would respond to holy or unholy blessings. His research found that sounds coupled with intention can restore water to its original vital source. That means holy water has sacred power if it was blessed, with proper intent. One of the secrets well-kept from the human race is that our emotions energize the God consciousness. Your emotions connect you to your spiritual body, allowing you to utilize logic and reason.

Life is like the pendulum of a large clock, as it swings in one direction it gains momentum to travel equal distance in another direction. It produces perpetual motion that will generate energy. Everything requires energy, which needs to be replaced when used. God is no exception, so humanity is the pendulum on the "GOD Clock."

Have you considered that crop circles are designed by geometric frequencies and are products of an unspoken universal symbolic language?

CHAPTER FITHTEEN

SINGING to YOURSELF

It was January 8, 2011, and like most citizens of the US, I was watching the National News that was reporting the shooting of U.S. Representative Gabrielle Giffords. She was critically wounded with a bullet on the left side of the brain. There were six dead and an additional thirteen wounded. That was a dark day for our government and our country with all of our hearts going out to the victims and their families. We all ask "WHY"? But of course, the answers are not simple.

Like everyone else, I followed this story with great interest and sent many well wishes with healing energy. I also lit candles for the favorable healing of all the victims. As the days passed the nation witnessed a miracle as Gabby started her long journey back to reality and living. Since the damage to her brain was in the left hemisphere, which is the headquarters for the storage of words, she lacked the ability to speak. That was until someone had the novel idea of singing to her, to which she responded in a favorable way. That might have been surprising to the medical profession, but not to her speech therapist Maegan Morrow. As Gabby's music therapist, she said, "The brain can heal itself if you do the right protocol."

According to clinical research, music is stored in the same area of the brain that invents our memory, emotions, and movement. Maegan also said. "If I play with a rhythm, I can affect the rest of the body. The body naturally aligns with a rhythm in the environment." So, it stands to reason the above statement could also read, "that the brain can heal its BODY if given the right protocol."

There is evidence that brain damaged patients can use singing to relearn speech and improve their thinking patterns. That proves the power of music and the importance of words. Gaddy's case has caused many, including myself, to show interest in researching the sound of music in the right brain.

The question was asked regarding Gabby, "If it is so difficult to speak a full sentence, why is it so simple for her to sing it?" The answer is that the left-brain specializes in words, and although it understands the music, it cannot give a musical recital. That is an act of creativity that belongs to right brain activity.

Music doesn't transport information about particular objects, although the lyrics might. Instead, it moves you with a type of emotion, that results in using the right hemisphere of your brain. The reason it works is that both sides of the brain can vocalize. And both can be involved in music, but only the right side can create the songs you sing. Your brain, either left or right responds more successfully to things it is familiar with, and labors when it is exposed to new information. That tells you that when you are making up the songs to sing to yourself, use a musical tune that you are familiar with. It will be easier to match your healing lyrics to the melody that already plays in your head. It also tells you that if the Right Brain can assist in reestablishing left-brain language, it can also reestablish left-brain health. The brain is a network of connections; the ones that get used get stronger, the ones unused will atrophy. So, start developing your brain, instead of watching left brain TV and soap operas, try constructive activities, take a walk or read a book. TV is great in moderation, but it has created a country of couch potatoes who are 99% left-brain dominated. Many are controlled by the subliminal advertising of the giant corporations that now rule our basic life habits and food intake. We have to collectively, first take control of ourselves then our environment along with the world we live in, without trying to enforce our religious and political opinions. Remember that Mother Nature is our playpen respect her, and she will take good care of you.

The fact that music can rewire the brain is fast becoming a clinically recognized possibility in our modern medical society. The doctors are interested, the public is skeptical, and the insurance companies say no, we do not cover it. It is the language you speak, and the music you make, that changes your programming. You can listen to music, and it has great value, but the music you make for yourself is what you need to change your health and life.

Singing in the brain is not something new, just forgotten. In the book "Musicophilia" by Dr. Sacks, he makes reference to an article by neurologist Dr. John H. Jackson 1871 titled, "Singing by Speechless [Aphasic] Children." In the 40's, music therapy was recognized as a tool of healing by our military, for the injured soldiers coming back from World War 11. That was the Melodic intonation therapy process used by music therapists which involves the rise and fall of the voice in speaking, or singing. These patients had communication disorders from a damaged left hemisphere of the brain. The right brain's interest in melodies took over, and communication was improved.

When Einstein was in his creative mood, he would play his violin and he made references to the fact that intuition came to him while he was playing. He suggested that there was a correlation between his music and an opening door He also suggested that a musical key unlocked the intuition area of the brain.

It is possible, and many people do, successfully sing in their head without uttering a sound. They can listen to entire melody, song or symphony in their head observing it's minutest detail. Beethoven composed his greatest works long after he became totally deaf. He must have heard the sounds in his head like we see and hear our dreams. He had the ability to compose in his head that which his physical ears could never hear.

We are a linguistic species, but the brain's ability to access speech cannot be limited to just speech alone. It must belong to any sound wave and incorporate all the sounds of nature. We are not the only singing specimens on earth. We are just the only ones that puts words to the music and create a song. That is not to say the birds, and other creatures do not sing a message.

I can walk a country mile and still be in my yard, and it is alive with sounds, especially at night. The loudest and most continuous one is the symphony of the insect world. It sounds like electric energy running through high power lines. Then there is the percussion section from the frog pond and an occasional drum roll from the hoot owls on the hill.

If music can access one part of the brain's activities, it can access all parts, especially those that deal with the health of your body. We should consider health the number one goal of our body because without it nothing else can be successful.

Billions of cells make up your body. Have you ever considered talking to them? Yes, you should talk or sing to your cells because they have cellular bio-consciousness.

Every cell is a living entity that is in search of fulfillment. The cells job is to complete your wishes, hopes, and desires, rejuvenate your body and keep you healthy. It accomplishes that with the cooperation of tissue and organ consciousness.

Your cells hold vast amounts of memory and experiences. They totally rebuild your body, cell by cell, approximately every seven years. So that reflection in your mirror this morning was not the same smile that greeted you eight years ago. We should feel younger each day, month and year of our life. But instead, we have been programmed from birth that you grow a year older each birthday and when you have a certain number of these special days you are old and should get ready to die. When a person dies, that means the spirit leaves the body, but the body is still very much alive because the cells can sometimes take days to die.

Each cell in your body has a limited lifespan. However, it has a rejuvenating ability to replace itself with a new one at a given time. It replaces itself with a new cell unless you are willing to accept a rebuilt or restored cell. If you have a cancer cell and you are not willing to insist on a new cell your brain thinks you like that cell, so gives you a new cancer cell. Start seeing your cells as organs and insist that all changes require only new cells or stem cells. Do this by creating yourself a song and sing it to the cells of your body.

There are several body cells that never, or rarely, exchange, so you must take good care of the ones you have or suffer the consequence. At birth your cerebral cortex is loaded with Neurons and if you waste them by abusing your brain, there are no replacements. Glial cells are the servants to these neurons as well as your nervous system, so sing an energy song in honor of your Glial cells, this will help you think. Your heart cells join this party as cells that take longer to replace.

Body cells do not all change at the same rate, and some are affected by your age, the older you are, the slower the exchange. Probably the fastest turnover are the cells that line your stomach as they last only five days. Skin cells also recycle quickly, because we watch a wound heal in a matter of days and have to clean continually the ring of dead cells that collect around the bathtub. Your red blood cells last an average of four months, while your liver cells stay with you for sixteen months. Even your skeletal structure rebuilds itself several times over your lifespan. We are a unit of proportional energy, so there is no reason for us to age and die.

I like to sing to my stem cells because they are the body's raw materials. They are cells that can generate into any body cell like a universal donor. They can generate new cell types and stand alone as the only body cell capable of performing that task. These cells are referred to as embryonic stem cells, because the body starts out with a cluster of them that divide into different types of body cells as it constructs your body. In my original song I use regression to return to my fetus or embryonic beginning. I retrieve my original cells because of their regenerative properties and abilities to repair diseased tissue and body parts.

It has been scientifically proven that some quantum particles are affected by nothing more that conscious observation. So, I am saying with confidence that conscious observation also affects your conscious effort to rejuvenate your body with the use of your original stem cells. When you intentionally regress yourself through self-hypnosis you interact with all the memories of your monad [original spark of life]. This can be on any plane of existence in any time frame. Since teleportation is a possibility, [the Philadelphia experiment which gave us proof] then bring those cells to the now and put them in your designated spot. If you lack confidence, tell your body to put them where they are needed.

Your body produces a limited amount of stem cells, known as Adult stem cells. Embryonic stem cells can change into over two hundred types of body cells whereas the adult cells are localized. So, it is best to use your original stem cells in your songs.

All cells are composed primarily of water. The body is 70% water, but different body parts have varying degrees of water volume. Your blood is 92% water, your brain along with muscle mass is 75% while your bone and fat are only 22%. Water is the most important substance you put into your mouth. So, sing blessings to the water you drink and take measures that it is the best you can give yourself.

I recommend that you read the books by Masaru Emoto, on the properties of water and ice crystals. From childhood, I have been fascinated with snowflakes and their original designs, as well as the designs of ice crystals that decorate my winter windows. We find that water is mesmerizing with mystical qualities as we interact with it in the form of vapor, liquid or solid. We steam our food; drink our tea, wash and swim in it. We stomp in puddles, run through raindrops, skip rocks on smooth ponds, and use it for numerous sports and outdoor activities. As steam, it has enough energy to drive trains and move mountains. As a liquid, it gives life to everything on earth as it forms rivers and decorates our landscapes and as ice, it preserves and renews.

We are over half water; So, it is important to research our water intake to stay healthy, by following a few rules. Do not drink water that has fluoride and additives in it, which is 100% of city tap water. Use a filter to clean out toxins and try not to drink water that has been in a plastic bottle.

In 1980, I entertained a fascinating personality who wore a saffron robe. This elderly monk was a keynote speaker at the conference we were hosting, and his subject matter was charging your water with color and sun energy. I cannot remember his name, but I remember his message. He said to use a clear glass with natural crystals. Use clear quartz or something amethyst. Fill your container with water and let it set in the sun all day then leave it out all night. Next morning it is pure and good to drink.

He said to start collecting colored glass bottles and use them as water containers. Do the same by filling them with water and sitting them in the sun. You may put clear crystals in them, but it is the color of the glass, you are also charging. Green charged water is antiseptic; Red is an energy drink while orange vitalizes and yellow cleanses, blue is a tranquilizer while purple lifts your spirits. I sometime expose my drinking water to storms as it absorbs the power of nature. Or to the influence of a Full moon or a certain day or the year. Water has power to learn how to utilize it.

If you put other rocks or minerals in the water, be sure they have not been contaminated, which will leave a side effect in the water.

When questioning, the logic and reasoning, behind singing to yourself, just ask one question. "Why do we light candles and sing hymns in the church?"

CHAPTER SIXTEEN

THE BRAIN

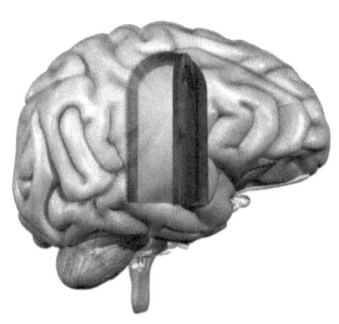

The scientific study of the human brain is based on the Darwinian theories of physical form. It leaves no room for the metaphysical assumption that spirit also occupies that same physical space. I claim no authority regarding the scientific world that has medically detailed the anatomy and activities of the brain. I do, however, claim to be an energetic, exuberant student of both physics and metaphysics regarding body, mind and soul. Scientists judge the brain in its physical form without much regard to the spiritual source that energizes it, leaving that part up to God. I give respect and appreciation to the classical approach but direct my information and theories to the separation of brain and mind in the metaphysical approach.

Regardless of the form of life, the number one function of the brain is survival. Being part of the animal kingdom we have a brain that helps us achieve that. So, it is our objective to teach our brain and assist it in better executing the functions it was so uniquely designed to perform. The human brain is the most sophisticated unit of energy in the scientific world. It is more intelligent than any computer in our existence although our laptop might disagree. We use such a small percentage of our brainpower and think we are a Genesis. If we did use it all we could be Gods.

The mechanics of the brain are directly related to our survival. It is not the size and strength that dictates the winner of the game; it is the superior brain with intellect and capacity for thought. Learning how to program this creative asset assists in its survival and this book is directed to help you do that, by understanding the simplicity of the things in our life that we have complicated.

The metaphysical approach of brain analogy predates all modern data, as it was the precursor of the great philosophical geniuses from ancient history. Plato believed that the true substance of life had to be spiritual and could reincarnate through a series of physical forms because physical was ephemeral, and spirit was eternal. He also believed that the physical was the imperfect copy of the spirit and argued for the immortality of the soul.

The mind has a sophisticated way of collecting and programming the brain. Some interactions are natural reflexes, and others are trained responses. You can utilize these abilities through learning how to control and use both in harmony with each other.

When we think of our brain, we usually relate it to how intelligent we are, but that is a secondary factor for having a brain. IQ is our ability to learn, and along with using logic and reason are learned responses.

In reality, our brain is our universal sensory organ and critical to our survival. Age is the unit of measurement used for gauging its functioning potential, while life experiences are the learning tools that program it. What you are today is the totality of these two factors. If this masterpiece mainly involves choices and decisions made by you, for you; then it is safe to say, 'you are a product of your own making.' Now if you choose to change your creation, it is all up to you.

Your brain is a library of memories, featuring all the events and things you have been exposed to in your lifetime. Review your past and understand that, who you are today, is based on this lifetime of experiences and choices you have made. The logic of it is that your library is there to mirror your future and to improve your strongest assets through redundancy. Your memory is fragile and as you age it is increasingly inaccurate causing you to construct your future with a faulty blueprint. By understanding how to control your thinking and recreate your memories you can fashion your future the way you choose instead of just letting it happen.

The evolutionary features that divide humans from other animals are thinking in concepts, speaking in tongues, forming symbols, writing a language and later retrieval abilities. By following this evolutionary diagram, you can create a new you. The concept is you have the ability to change anything about yourself by first creating the change in your mind then planting it in your brain and visualize it in reality. Physically we are a product of evolution, and scientifically, we can follow that through the development of the human spine and brainstem that we share with reptiles and other animals.

It is not my intention for this book to be a manual on brain anatomy. But I will give you a condensed view of the basic brain structure. Your brain weighs 3% of your body weight and uses 20% of all your energy while producing enough electricity to light a bulb. Now, let's look at the brain from the bottom up, the way energy flows into it. Starting with the spinal cord, hindbrain, midbrain, and forebrain. The basic function of the hindbrain is to tend to all the bodies automatic needs, like the heart beating, lungs breathing, and intestines digesting. Then going up the brainstem there is the medulla oblongata, the pons, and the midbrain. These parts route information of the brain's sensory nerves coming in and motor nerves going out. Next is the Cerebellum that is the motor controller of body functions, along with motion memory, and body coordination. Above that are the Thalamus and the Hypothalamus, which sit on top of the brain stem. The

Thalamus distributes information and re-routes it to needed areas, while the Hypothalamus is credited with, maintaining body temperature. The posterior pituitary gland stems from here and produces hormones like oxytocin and diuretics.

Then for the mass of the brain you have the cerebrum that integrates billions of neurons and synapses that allow us to make sense of information as we get it. The two-hemispheres, left for mathematical reasoning, words and speech, the right for creative thought singing music and facial recognition. These two are connected by a band of nerves called the corpus callosum. The Basal Ganglia is just below the corpus callosum, and it is made up of nuclei that are bunches of neurons that have the same function. In this area, but not actually a part of the brain, is the location of the pineal gland.

We crown ourselves with the Frontal lobe, which is the part that gives us higher concepts with intuitive abilities and designates us as a human. Next comes the parietal lobe for logic and reason and the occipital lobe on the back of your head for vision with temporal lobes on either side for hearing. Lastly, there are two reigns bordering the frontal and parietal called the somatosensory cortex coming into the Parietal lobe and the motor cortex information going out of the Frontal lobe.

Now, let us look at the part of the brain that I find most interesting. The energy part, or the brainwaves, cannot be put in a petri dish, cannot be dissected, cannot be transplanted, but can be measured and altered. I'm quite sure that you have all heard the statement that someone has, "BATS IN THE BELFRY." It is an antiquated saying with insanity and madness as its target. We might call someone Batty,' if we think they are, in our opinion, not mentally sound. However, in my opinion, this saying has the same intrigue as hiding the truth of the pineal gland on the back of our dollar bill. Secrets are best hidden in plain sight, and those who recognize them will understand.

The brain waves are Beta, Alpha, and Theta. I just spelled BAT, so of course we all have Bats in our Belfry. The other two brain waves are Gamma and Delta and putting your soul between these you have GOD. "I am that I am, I AM GOD". In all esoteric teachings your soul is a 0, in the Tarot the 0 is the fool that represents your incarnating soul. I am working on an upcoming book on 'The TAROT' that takes this concept into great detail along with the connection between the gamma wave and the pineal gland.

Everyone displays these waves to differing degrees, and you can learn to control these waves by meditation and other biofeedback methods. The most important and least developed in most people is the Gamma and its connection to the Delta. Simply put you talk to your God in your sleep through the pineal gland.

Your brain waves are like one big family and if they do

not commute properly and function in a compatible environment they create disharmony in the body, which creates disease. Brainwaves do not compete with each other because one is not more important than another. An EEG will measure all these brain waves at the same time because they are continuous, but only one of them can dominate at any point in time.

If you have a conscious life, you must display brain waves. They can be measured with an EEG that gives a recording of their frequencies. It measures the electrical activity the mind creates when it goes from thinking to sleep, or a good mood to a bad one. Within the neurons of the brain, a measurable current flow through the skull that is recorded, on medical instruments. This is used along with many other procedures such as MRI and CT's to diagnose forms of illness, from a stroke, coma, sleep apnea and many more. It is often used, as the defining point in a brain dead patient.

The electrical signals in your brain oscillate through the nerve cells and fire in a pattern called brainwaves. The waves are connected to your biological chemistry and reflect your thoughts, moods, emotions and state of awareness. You are what you think, and your thoughts can be measured through sound wave technology. Different frequencies are identified with varying states of consciousness.

When we are wide awake, we are in Beta and vibrate at 16

to 31 Hz, so even being awake there is a different degree of wakefulness. Beta is associated with all normal daily functions including fear, stress, anger, mood swings, anxiety, as well as love and happiness. There are three sections to the Beta wave classified as low, medium, and high Beta. In low you might do too much daydreaming, in high Beta you are close to Gamma and get insights and new ideas but could also feel anxiety.

When you relax, your brain goes into Alpha, 8-15 Hz, this is the state of meditation and can be used to strengthen memory and learning. This is a calm state where you can relax your problems and just melt away. It is a peaceful place, where you can consciously organize your life. When you think someone has their head in a cloud, they are in the state of Alpha.

Next, you go into Theta, 4-7 Hz, on your way to total relaxation when the world disappears, and you feel like just floating away. It is in this state, if you are aware and listening, you can get insight and inspiration; it helps improve your creativity and intuition. If you learn to explore this dream-like wonderland you can do almost anything you wish and become anything you want. This is where meditation opens up the magic of the Gamma waves. Theta is light sleep when you are almost asleep, but not really awake.

When you go to sleep, your brain is in Delta brainwave that is 0.1-3 Hz. Here, you go into a deep dreamless sleep. It is here that all growth and healing take place, when the body is at rest it can repair itself. Because of this body building quality, the delta wave is more active in babies and young children. These waves are related to unconscious body functions like breathing and heartbeat. This is why sleep is so important, and the need increases with old age. REM [rapid eye movement] sleep is most important for rebuilding a sound body.

Gamma waves [32-100Hz.] are the newest find in our medical world and some institutions still do not recognize their true value. These waves are involved in learning, advance concepts, and processing higher tasks. They are closely associated with our senses and could be called the director of our 6th sense of intuition and insight. Gamma waves are fast and complex. They are like the frequency of a flute. Could that be why the mythological Pan plays the flute?

Recent research shows that the pineal gland can become activated through deep meditation that takes place in the Gamma wave range. The objective is to unlock higher psychic abilities. Relaxation music is a good place to start or better still, start humming yourself. The Gamma wave covers as much area as three times the total of the accumulative basic waves, so in my opinion that is a lot of unexplored area. Exercising and expanding is the name of this brain game.

There are many opinions about what frequency each brain

wave lives on, so I am using the Wikipedia version of Hz. values.

Gamma wave – (32 – 100 Hz) Meditations will improve higher consciousness.

Beta wave – (16 – 31 Hz) Wake up with Coffee or energy drinks helps here.

Alpha wave – (8 – 15 Hz) Relaxation, self-hypnosis and visualization happen here.

Theta wave – (4 – 7 Hz) Recreational stimulants greatly affect this area.

Delta wave – (0.1 – 3 Hz) Deep Sleep, REM Sleep and Dreams for learning.

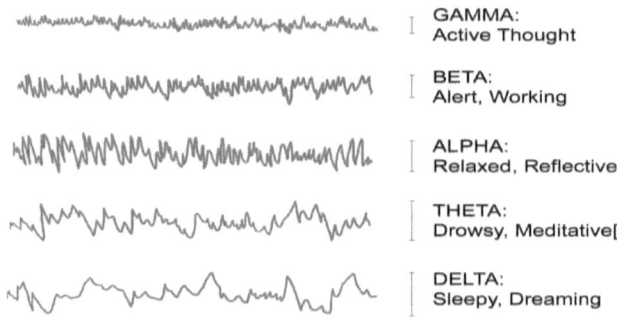

GAMMA: Active Thought
BETA: Alert, Working
ALPHA: Relaxed, Reflective
THETA: Drowsy, Meditative[
DELTA: Sleepy, Dreaming

When you are wide-awake and your most alert you are in Beta, [16 – 31 Hz]. High frequency, low amplitude waves that we activate in our daytime life. If you do not have enough of them, you have difficulty concentrating, if you have too many you have anxiety. When you are active, in conscious thought, anxious, and wide-awake you are functioning in Beta stage.

Changing brain waves:
Any change in routine activity changes brain activity. Chemical intervention also changes brain and body correlation. So, remember that when you take those pills, either recreationally or by prescription, 'Do you really want to do that to your body?' You have the choice.

The Internet is a great place to find brainwave entertainment and neurofeedback. I enjoy fractals on YouTube.com, I get totally lost in the colors and movement and usually mute the sound.

CHAPTER SEVENTEEN

COLOR

We live in an ocean of perpetual colored substance that is necessary for our existence. The sun and the moon alter these ingredients while continually stirring this soup. Although you might just take it for granted without much consideration that the sky is blue, and the grass is green. The real fact is our ocean is the atmosphere, and the life-giving substance is air and light. When light energy meets air, its molecules become excited, and nitrogen and oxygen are released giving us life.

Although both are invisible, they are also visible, for we can see the motion of the air and the color of the light. The light gives life energy that rides on the spectrum of colors feeding our senses. By utilizing a triangular prism and a light ray from the sun, you can divide the colors into a rainbow. Or Mother Nature can do it and call it 'God's bow of promise.' Gen: 9:13 KJV "I do set my bow in the cloud, and it shall be for a token of a covenant between me and the earth."

In the songs I sing to myself, I utilize the rainbow energy. I bathe myself with it when singing in the shower. I expose myself to it when I salute the sun at sunrise. I encourage its essence when I meditate and focus on its colors when I visualize. I also created a rainbow diet for myself because eating bright colored foods is beneficial to your daily wellbeing.

You are a Prism; your body is the prism of light and life, and as you face the morning rays of the sun, you turn on your natural spectral abilities. They are called Chakras, and they line up with the Kundalini power points that energize life. So, the 'bow of promise' given to mankind is to be able to function in a higher consciousness by awakening Kundalini power and activating the pineal gland. History symbolically shows us this self-knowledge in the form of the serpent wisdom of the Caduceus.

The Caduceus predates our written text and belongs to the pre-anthropomorphic era. It was the staff carried by the Greek God Hermes, who inherited it from the God Harold and gave it to Mercury the messenger of the Gods. It is often mistaken, for the Rod of Asclepius that has only one snake. The true representation is the Caduceus with two snakes intertwined on a straight staff capped with a pinecone. It is pictured in the Egyptian hieroglyphics as well as in ancient, classical and modern art forms.

During WWII, the U.S. military adopted the symbol as meaning Medical, and it has since migrated into the professional field of medicine as a symbol that legitimizes the medical world. The Veterinarian aspect of medicine then started using the Rod of Asclepius with one snake as their symbol of authority. The Caduceus has two snakes forming the DNA double helix. These two strands go in opposing directions in an anti-parallel fashion so that the snakes face each other at the top of the staff, capped with a pinecone for the pineal gland. Often the staff is shown with a pair of wings. Usually carried in the left hand of the hero showing that it belongs to the right hemisphere activity of the brain. The snakes are symbolic of hidden wisdom, giving the message that they are protecting the mysteries of the pinecone they balance on their staff. All this belongs to Color because the Sun's energy focused through the prism of self, activates the rainbow Chakras to open your single eye.

What are chakras?
A chakra is a spinning vortex or wheel of colored energy. It is part of the Kundalini that shadows your spinal column. Consisting of seven chakras in the seven colors of the rainbow and linking up with seven vital areas they energize your body. Your physical body digests and processes physical food for energy while the chakras

digest invisible emotional food like love, ambitions and accomplishments into energy that likewise feeds your body. Your body has numerous chakras, but there are seven that are the prime energy points of the body.

When you view a rainbow from your backyard the color red is on the top and the color purple on the bottom, but your Chakras are colored the other way around with red on the bottom. To put yourself in the proper position for the natural-colored spectrum to line up with the chakras you must first realize that the rainbow is a circle. It is a matter of perspective that we see it as a bow.

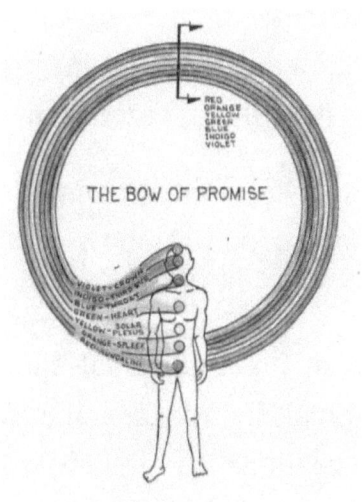

In my drawing of 1989 [From my video Crystals flowers of the Earth] I show that by placing yourself, in the lower part of the bow, as the microcosm of the macrocosm, your chakras line up properly with the colors of the spectrum.

I have chased rainbows all my life and will continue until I die. They excite my psyche and bring out that child within that keeps me young and energized. If you want to dance with a rainbow, it is simple. Rainbows form at 40 to 45 degrees of either sunrise or sunset. You will need a garden hose with a fine spray nozzle and the willingness to get wet. Put your back to the sun and start playing with the spray and you can play one of my favorite games, skip the bow. The reflections you create are mostly in circles so if you are limber enough try for a hula-hoop.

Rainbows are an optical illusion that ride on water droplets and come into reality by observation based on perspective. They also utilize spray and mist, especially from waterfalls. Some of my most cherished memories of rainbows come from the numerous times I have visited Niagara Falls. The sound of the raging water is so loud that it excites your adrenaline. This amplifies the visional effects, depending on the brightness of the sun and the time of day you are being entertained by the dancing color of the magic of Niagara. That is my kind of entertainment.

The sky inside the rainbow is always brighter than the sky on its outer rim, and if there is a second rainbow on this outside rim, it will be in reverse color in lighter shades.

The spring of 1989 found me in my traditional spot at Scarborough Renaissance Festival in Waxahachie TX, selling my original jewelry creations to the eccentric patrons that dared to be different. Mother Nature seems to follow the same paths when she decides to take a wild ride on a tornado, and the location of these festival grounds are one of her favorite party spots. She recently took out the back half or the grounds and later came back to try it again, only that time she jumped the grounds, hitting downtown Waxahachie. This date in memory was surrounded with that similar attitude of the Great Mother, and all fair going patrons could feel something strange in the air, just knowing that she was about to kick our butts again.

Anxiety rose to panic heights as those creepy dark storm clouds folded in on us. The winds were wild, and everyone was trying to stand up straight and hang on to their belongings while mothers grabbed their kids. The pressure grew to explosive heights, and suddenly the winds stopped. The world went silent, and I took a sigh of relief. Looking up I could see that all eyes were focused at twelve o'clock high in the sky. Some patrons fell on their knees; others clasp their hands in prayer while other just stared in amazement. I could hear shouts that "God is Coming." "This is the Day of Judgment," "Jesus is coming back." "Revelation has started coming true," and, of course, many more.

DÉJÀ VU. If I am not mistaken, I think I have been here before, and it is called the Eye of the storm. The reality of the day was that, directly overhead, high in the darkened sky, was an opening of a sunny sky in a perfect circle. Surrounding that hole and framed by darkness, there was the most beautiful full circle rainbow that I had ever seen. The colors were so vivid you could taste them, and you knew you had just been blessed. The area was a vacuum of hollow silence as the viewers, out of fear or praise, watched this grand finality. It stayed at that location in full dress for at least ten minutes, and I watched as it faded into nothingness. I often visit that memory in my library while doing visualization meditation. I sample each color for sound and flavor, wrap myself in the color and feel it's life while smelling its comfort. It was as if you could teleport, through that circle in the sky, and become physically rejuvenated. It was a portal into an alternative existence.

The summer of the 90's was one of those outrageous weather seasons. I was traveling from Sheridan Wyoming south toward Casper, and the sky was a stage show of lightning, orchestrated by the sound of thunder and crashing of clouds. A little rain and a lot of open sky for the rainbows that followed, little more rain, lots of lightening and some of the most beautiful full bows with second and even third bows. Nature reverses the color each time she repeats the same rainbow so it in interesting to view the reflections of the sister bows.

We all know that a picture is worth 1000 words so here is a drawing by

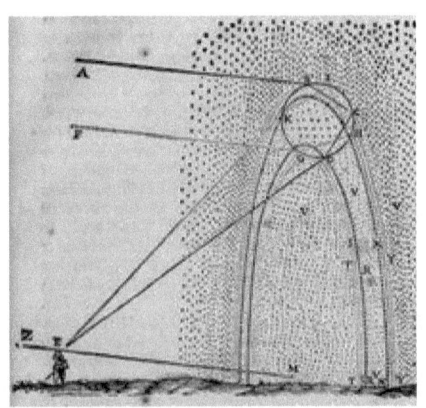

Rene Descartes 1637 from his sketchbook of 'Discourse on Methods,' shows how it works. This concert lasted all day with minor intermissions, as evening was approaching, I was

outside Denver, headed toward St Louis. The sun was sitting behind me, and I was driving through bright sunlight. The storm front loomed like a black form in front of me. It was a wall, which looked as solid as a rock and as large as a mountain. It reflected the largest, brightest, most vivid colored rainbow I had ever been close to. The color were reflecting off the storm front. I had driven through fog banks before, which can be deadly, and this looked similar. The traffic was slow, and as I approached the wall the rainbow got larger. It has been stated that a rainbow cannot be physically approached, but this one was reflected from a storm barrier, so I think the rules changed. As I got closer to the color, I was looking for the pot of gold, and then I went through the rainbow. When this happened, I realized that the pot of gold at the end of the rainbow was the thrill of passing through it. I received unknown energy and the thrill of the moment. I also videoed it.

In July 2010, I was flying from Cleveland, Ohio to Fayetteville, Arkansas, which required a flight change in Chicago. As luck would have it, I landed in Chicago just fine but storms in the area had canceled my flight to Fayetteville. At the last minute, I hitchhiked a flight into Springfield Missouri that would do just fine in getting me home.

The sun was just setting, as we took off, and the flight was 90 minutes. Once we were about 15 minutes into the trip, I spotted a magical spot in the sky that entertained me for the remainder of the trip. There was just enough sun in the west, to highlight the clouds. The ones to the east were unfriendly. Nested in these unfriendly clouds was a circle rainbow over a pocket of lightning flashes. We were flying above this storm. Looking down on it was like viewing a theater in the round with a fish bowel effect. It was a never-ending stream of flashes of many types of lightning. It was like watching fireworks for an hour; I watched in wonderment until we were far past the storm.

Light is energy and color is matter; when they interact, they produce wavelengths of frequencies that we can utilize as a healing substance. Your mind can absorb these and weave, and thread them through your body.

The ancients were well versed in Chromo therapy, known as light therapy. Today's world of alternative medicine practitioners, including myself, uses these techniques that are unveiled from our legends of hieroglyphic, clay tablets and rock art. A new modification of the title is 'Vibrational' medicine because it has more of a Quantum tone.

It involves the use of color in many forms, as in gemstones and crystals from the mineral kingdom, and plants and flowers from the vegetable world. Sunlight and sound form our electromagnetic energy, along with your imagination, form the Quantum knowledge of the future. There are endless other ways of utilizing color and shades of color such as candles, drinks, clothing, wall paint, etc.

Ancient Egyptians utilized colored glass walls exposed to the sun as solarium rooms to achieve therapeutic properties from colored light magic. This influence later traveled to the Houses of God, cathedrals, churches, and temples, as stained-glass windows. Although the religious influence lost the real meaning of the stained glass windows and considered them only as a part of their influential décor, they still maintained their subliminal healing power. The Bible makes hundreds of references to colors and the way they should be used.

Color therapy is being recognized today in many forms of professional healing under the disguise of clinical terms. A recent example was on CNN where they brought to national attention, the fact that by using a blue light on the backs of knees, you could adjust the body clock to overcome jet lag. They also suggested other situations that this treatment could be effective, such as night workers and shift sleep problems.

It is a proven fact that lack of color from light causes seasonal depression [SAD]. It has always been a fact that by putting an ill person outside in fresh air and sunshine they feel better. Exposing them to the influence of controlled color, can and has often healed them.

When someone says 4th of July, what is the first thought that goes through your mind? The 99.9% correct answer would be fireworks, and then the Holiday off from work. A few might say Independence Day, but sadly half of them cannot tell you from what we are independent. The part they remember is the fireworks because of the excitement; the noise and the magic or the exploding colors.

This same excitement in color magic can be yours on YouTube in the form of Fractals. I give myself a daily Fractal fix and love it. I have been told they are ten cents short of LSD and next door to psychedelics. Having never been involved in that social activity I cannot make that a personal statement. I find Fractals very useful in Meditation and Visualization as they have a hallucinogenic effect. I love the colors and their movement as they entertain my mind. I find them equally useful in what I do for myself as well as my clients, by having them watch the screen for several minutes before their secession. I believe that doctor's waiting rooms should substitute the TV for YouTube Fractals.

You should investigate the use of fractals before you make it a habit because like all good things there are persons that try to spoil the positive effect with subliminal inserts. Be careful that you choose the positive ones to watch. For the most part, I cannot tolerate the sound that comes with them, so I mute the TV and sit in silence or play my brainwave music.

Now what is a fractal? It is a never-ending design of a photograph of a quantum sound partial. It is the repetition of and recording of the feedback over and over like the mirror or mirror scene. There are complicated formulas that give the recipe of each design. Fractals might remind you of the hippy's tie-died T-shirt or a Grateful Dead poster but it is not a cultural design, but rather features the nature and our DNA. A true fractal captures the essence of nature and simplifies its complex designs to shows the similarities of our connection to all the parts of nature.

Think of a fractal as a hand full of STUFF. Then divide it in two and you have two hands filled with stuff, then continue dividing and you always have hands filled of stuff, and regardless how many times you divide this quantum stuff, it is still stuff. It is everlasting stuff; it is endless stuff. Now photograph the trail of this endless division of stuff and you have fractals. It always looks like stuff. When color is added it is colored stuff.

The laws controlling fractals are found in nature and cosmic geometry in the formula of the golden mean, which is 1.618. It is a ratio that is utilized in nature as the golden rectangle. TRUE Fractal designs come from nature, so look at the form of the tree and branches. They look alike and branches match the root system that you cannot see because it is below the ground. Then look closer and see where each branch starts, you have the same design of another tree, then look even closer and see that branch has shoots of the same design. Now look at your body and see the heart that is the base of the tree with the veins as branches that go into smaller veins, then smaller veins, etc. They look the same regardless of the size. Now are you getting the connection of how all things in nature are the same?

Follow the pattern of electricity. It looks like the root structure of any plant or your vascular system, or the path the river makes on the earth, or the veins in a simple leaf. You can find fractals in a drop of water, an ice crystal, a pinecone, a sunflower; everything you look at has fractal forms. So, look at things differently and see your microscopic self in all things.

There is a reason I am supposed to attempt to understand the value of this equation. In 2003 I knew nothing about 1.618, that is until I got a new cell phone and that happened to have 1618 as the last four numbers of my phone. A few months later I lost my mother. All six siblings gathered to pay respect and honorably say our goodbyes to the person that had shaped our lives. As in all situations like this, there was mundane business that had to be dealt with and properties to be disposed of, so I ended up with mother's car. On the 2000-mile trip home, my sister and her husband, who also live in Missouri, followed me. She was reading "Dan Brown's Da Vinci Code" while he drove. We pulled into a rest area, and she pointed out what Brown had to say about the magic of 1618 and also, that the plates on mother's car were 1618.

According to authorities in history that go back over 2.400 years including Pythagoras, Leonardo and Kepler, it is the key to understanding the construction of all things in nature. It has been analyzed for centuries and now we are fortunate in being able to view it because Dr. Benoit Mandelbrot discovered how to photograph a mathematical equation.

To explore this magical start with the Mandelbrot set or the Julia set because they are the originals. Dr. Benoit Mandelbrot [1924-2010], in 1975 published, Les Objects Fractals and later several other books on the Mathematics of Fractals. His autobiography, 'The Fractalist', was published in 2012. He was part of the research division of IBM where he developed his magic from cosmic geometry and gave it the name Fractal. He is known as the Father of Fractals, and The Mandelbrot set was named in his honor. Fractals are the foundation of the computer-drawn illustrations and magical Special effects of the movie industry.

Today's computer animation is made possible by the Dr. Mandelbrot's insight into the mathematical magic of forms in nature. Many movies use computer graphics of one kind or another to make life-like imagery, from Star Wars to Jurassic Park. These action movies that give you the 'Excitement of the Chase' are made possible by fractal generated computer graphics. [CGI] Fractals are the heartbeat of storm predictions and seismology. They are used to analyze such things as population statistics, science, and medical studies and technology. We must give recognition to the little-known fact that this one man has affected everyone on the planet.

In my opinion, because of its connection to all things in nature, and thus creation, it has true magic. So, I have my daily exposure to this magic and often leave it running on my TV all day to filter the influence into my home and environment.

Rainbow Meditation

Find a comfortable spot, perhaps your favorite recliner and just lay back and fold into it. Just relax and take a deep breath, in through the mouth and out through the nose. Once again in through the mouth and out through the nose and this time feel more relaxed. Now a third time and you are starting to feel the relaxation as a warmth goes from the bottom of your feet to the top of your head. Focus on how your body feels, become aware of your entire body, knowing you have each toe and all the way to having each finger. Realize you have two legs and two arms and relax that body, become so relaxed that you cannot feel that you have these body parts. Then, notice that you have a head that has two eyes that are shut, and two ears that you cannot shut. Now listen to yourself and hear your breath then listen to your heartbeat. While aligning yourself to that rhythm, you are going to take a walk through the park on a beautiful afternoon. It is just after a cool rain, and the sun peeks over the clouds and produces a beautiful rainbow. You paused in its reflection and absorbed its beauty and its colors.

RED

From the bottom of the bow, you see Red, the color of life, the red blood that flows through your veins. Red is energy that fosters life and forgives aggression. Red is the great energizer that is the Mother of vitality. It stimulates your creative and excites your procreative abilities. It is the universal color for danger, and it is your built in stop signal with a warning never to see red. This color is courageous, passionate and strong, but can be rebellious and obstinate. So breathe in all that the color red can give you and deliver it to your base chakra. It is referred to as the root chakra and is located at the base of the spine known as the pelvic floor. It occupies the bottom three vertebrate. It grounds you, giving you stability in life.

This chakra feeds the adrenal glands with energy to control your body's blood-flow and its quality. It is related to the adrenal glands that control adrenalin and body temperatures. It creates warmth to ease and release rigidity on leg movement and related activities. It is red for passion, and sexual excitement and when diluted it becomes softened to pink as it focuses on love as in self-love and respect as well as creativity.

ORANGE

Now, move up and tap in on the beautiful color of Orange, the child of red and yellow. It inherits the warmth from yellow and the energy from red to become a powerful healing color. It is a mental color of enthusiasm and thinking, it compliments your creativity. It is the color of excitement; it has vitality and is a spontaneous health rejuvenator. It deals with personal emotions related to its red parent and its pride and vanity related to its yellow parent. It is a blend of appetite and fulfillment that adds ambition to wisdom.

Collect this color and plant it in the second chakra where it supplies energy to the colon and digestive processes. It assists with respiration and activates the thyroid, and shows us how to control our emotions. Orange acts as our body's sponge as it filters out toxins. This physical energy and mental wisdom announce their presence to the world with the first rays of the morning sun. These orange rays carry energy across the yellow sky to sit with red waves in the evening.

YELLOW

Now smile and bathe yourself in Yellow, the color of the sun and the blessings of the god of life. It is the color straight from heaven as its golden beams penetrate your mind and stimulate your higher mental abilities. It soothes pain as it warms the soul and allows mental release. It controls the liver and the gallbladder, and the stomach and spleen, all the activity of the body under the diaphragm. It is optimism, intelligence and inspiration and the rays of life energy.

Collect the yellow and move it to your third chakra called the Solar Plexus; the throne of your emotions and the power of your ego. The lust for life rises out of the solar plexus along with the pain of failure and the disappointment from loss. It promotes cheerfulness, flexibility, and curiosity.

GREEN
Now, balance yourself on the color green, the giver of life, love, and self-value. It is the color of nature and growth and productivity. It is a color that disinfects and neutralizes. Green brings renewal and restores a sense of well-being while balancing your heart and your emotions. It restores depleted energy and gives you a positive attitude. Green is the color of 'Go' and gives knowing of right and wrong, and the ability to recognize the difference. It is a friendly color since it is in the center on the spectrum, it can harmonize comfortably either up or down.

Now take your collection of green energy to your fourth chakra of the heart. It is an emotional color of real love, the feeling of belonging. Green is calming and healing as it stimulates growth. Green in this chakra creates equilibrium between the heart and the head and restores depleted energy. It is the Heart chakra, and the Green creates a natural pacemaker to harmonize with its environment. Green is calming and used as an institutional color of wellness.

BLUE
Reach out and draw in the blue, it is the Communications color. Let it talk to you. It is a cool color that refreshes

and follows loyalty as 'being true blue'. It is a shy color and sometimes is connected with depression or having the blues. It represents confidence, security, and organization. We think of peace, tranquility, and relaxation with blue skies and soft floating clouds giving us the feeling of freedom. Blue advances our spiritual perspective and represents holiness.

Attach the blue color to your fifth chakra, that is the Throat and your means of communication, spiritual as well as physical. It endorses truth in expression either in form or word. It lends conversation to the clairvoyant that hides behind your ego. It faces the truth in self through self-expression. Blue is the spectrum's astringent, with blue light therapy becoming very popular in the medical profession. It is being used for fever, high blood pressure, calms emotions, and anger. Any injury in the sports world is being addressed with the blue light.

INDIGO
Touch the color of Indigo and collect compassion and understanding. It is the great color for purification as it cleanses your blood. It is here that universal love connects to the forces of the universe and where inner knowledge makes a difference. This is where you see, rather than just look, and respect the difference between curiosity and knowledge. It is with indigo that wholesome becomes individualized, and your mind becomes the hologram of life.

This color belongs to your sixth chakra that is your third eye center. It sits just above the brow in the center of your head between your two eyes. It is the pineal gland, which is the seat of your soul, the connection of physical to invisible or body and mind. It governs perception of self-values and your relationship with your god self. It is that Holy Spirit portion of your god-Self.

VIOLET

Now absorb the Violet, the color of universal energies and inhale the color of spirituality. It activates your inspiration in life and living while motivating the quantum aspects of self. It gives the liberty of expansion of self while fulfilling responsibilities of life. It represents the future, constructed on the past while questioning our daily existence. It relates to the fantasy of the dream world while enhancing your psychic abilities. It is the awakening of spiritual awareness as the highest color on the spectrum. It is the intuition color and being connected to universal awareness, it transmits new ideas and information.

Move that color to the Seventh Chakra the crown of your head. This Chakra is also considered golden, It is the gate of the soul's entry at birth and exit at death. It is your Holy of Holies, your inner sanctuary; this is where your Arc of the Covenant is housed, giving you the ability to communicate with your God Self.

Think about the word 'Life' and feel life energy in your body as you spin your spiraling caduceus, activating your rod of life. See the energies of the colors wrap like coiled snakes of DNA inspired vitality out the top of your head, exploding the colors of light into your Aura. Now take a deep breath and be happy with yourself that you took a meditative trip through the rainbow and ended up loving yourself.

AURA

Color is a symptom of a disease or dis-ease in your body. It can be physical mental or emotional, and it changes your colors. This fact has been known since the beginning of time. You do not need to be professional to notice that if your friend is in the red with a flushed face, it usually means an elevated body temperature.

The aura is the energy field that surrounds everything that has life, from an insect, a leaf or a human. It is a way of seeing life. It can be photographed with the use of Kirlian photography. The aura looks like an egg around the entire body. It has nine energy layers of differing degrees of density that merge in a fashion similar to those in the rainbow, as one blends with the next. Your individual layers vary in depth and clarity, without merging as they overlay each other while occupying the same space. It might take practice, but you can see these fields with the naked eye. The layers relate to the chakras and share color correlation when it comes to seeing illness and body functions. From the body outward the fields graduate in density and vibration or frequency. The two outside fields are Quantum, and thus highly spiritual. When you see the aura, it pulsates in an energy pattern that makes the colors lighter or brighter.

Although the aura has been viewed by the eye since antiquity, it was impossible to photograph so we had to wait for Kirlian photography to be developed. In 1939, Semyon Kirlian accidentally discovered an object on a photographic plate in a high voltage experiment, but he was not aware of what he had stumbled on until 1970. It was then that Lynn Schroeder and Sheila Ostrander published their book, "Psychic Discoveries Behind the Iron Curtain."

It was a big deal when it hit the public and, of course, I had to have one of the first copies. Although, at that time, I did not know much about it and was eager to learn anything that came from Russians and was considered Psychic. Kirlian photography became a rage in the 70's, influential in the 80's and taken for granted after that. The impressive feature about Kirlian photography is it will photograph missing parts of an object. If you are missing a finger on your hand and take a photo of your hand, it will show the missing finger. So, what is it photographing, your hand or your memory?

RED
When seen in the Aura, it could mean Anger, willpower,

anxiety, and energy. It is a color you need to watch, you need red for energy, but because it has the lowest frequency, it is closely connected with your animal self and your survival instincts show up here. Red in the aura can also be an indicator of pain or injury. If colors show lighter, like red turns to pink, it has introduced compassion into the ingredient. Lust turns to Love. Anger turns to understanding.

ORANGE

If you have an abundance of orange in your aura, you have the urge to be creative and independent. It gives you the ability to do it yourself, which gives you self-satisfaction. Too much orange you want to live in your head with the need to protect and survive. Orange helps you plan activities and maintain organization.

YELLOW

In the aura, yellow inspires mental activity and calms the nerves. It will be dull in color if you have liver or stomach issues. Yellow is a golden color, so we place great value on it as an energy to lean on, as a form of logic. In your aura, it adds optimism, caution, cheerfulness, concentration and youth.

GREEN

When green is seen in the aura, it is connected with the heart and the lungs and as long and it is not muddy it represents wellness, stability, and energy. If it leans to the turquoise shades, it involves the immune system. More to the blue it would relate to the throat and the thyroid. Being the color of nature, it would amplify fertility, sincerity and efficiency. Seen in the aura, it could relate to blood pressure and heart conditions.

BLUE

Blue in the aura is a protective color that motivates service to others with love and affection, that has the ability to express emotion. Blue is the most emotional color making it easy to cry, or to become too blue and that generates illness. Blue is calm and caring, sensitive, with balance and contentment. It is the color of communication in voice and feelings with a mild way to express them.

INDIGO

Indigo is a color that gets lost, and no one remembers it exists. You have three primary colors: red, yellow, and blue. You have three secondary colors; orange, green, and purple. Now, how does indigo fit in? I falls between blue and purple, an area of wavelengths where the human eye has problems differentiating hues.

It was Isaac Newton in the mid-1660s, that decided indigo was a color that appears in the rainbow and in the band of color from his prism. He then added it to the colors in his spectrum and there it sits. Its aura is the visible side of ultraviolet or X-ray, making it a powerful though often unseen color in your aura.

PURPLE

Purple is the color of the divine spirit, and measures itself in the brightness of the crown in the seventh chakra. It tops the head like the aurora borealis tops the earth with its radiant colors dancing out the apex of your body. When you are healthy, they are vivid and excite the body, and when they are dull or muddy, you are ill. The reason can often be discerned by which colors are shades of gray and which are showing bright.

These colors are not considered spectral but are still important colors

BLACK

Black has completely absorbed all light, thus it is all possible colors. Black is the original color used by the human race for rock art and cave paintings, then came red. In the early Christian era, black became the color worn by royalty, clergy and anyone of importance. It still distinguishes the best dressed man at the party in a black suit and tie, alone with sophistication of being the lady in black. Also our legal judges that wear black robes, and of course the FBI and their 'men in black'. While it is put in the position of greatness, black has its opposite side. It is the color of negative: violence, black magic, wicked witches, mourning and a long list that I will not go into. In my opinion, history could not determine if black was good or bad so they gave it to both God and the Devil.

Psychologically, black is where you hide because there is no light, thus there is no self. It also represents strength and the ability to do as you please. All paper mistakes can be hidden by black ink.

When light appears, black releases all its colors, and finds that light is the only thing it cannot hide from.

WHITE

White is total, complete, innocent, and purity. Psychologically, it is wiping the slate clean and thus is a new start. It is an equal balance of all colors and shades of colors. It gives you a clean canvas and a full pallet to create as you choose. New opportunities come from White, as it is considered nothing and nothing contains everything. With white we are totally exposed and there is no hiding and the only color that can conquer it is black. It is purity in our thoughts, comfort in our emotions, superiority in our spirituality, strengthening in our energy and refreshing in our attitude. All that is delivered to us daily, free shipping, by the sun. Collect it and use it to keep yourself healthy.

SILVER

This is feminine energy and is connected to the moon where it generates emotion, sensitivity and versatility. It is the color of reflection, making you look within to really see your true self. It is reincarnation, rebirth and the cycles of life, which are the gifts of the Mother.

GOLD

The color coveted by all the Gods, cherished by their children and hoarded by the greedy. It represents success, luxury, elegance, achievement and value. We link it with love and roses, competition and the winner, with purple for royalty, with white for spirituality and in advertising we trust. It is the masculine energy powered by the sun. It is the color of absolute authority, financial richness and world power.

My Rainbow song

Go to the rainbow, collect the hues,
All of its colors from reds to blue.
Put them in by body that I may use,
Put them in my Chakras that I may know,
Put them in my Aura so that it may glow,
Put them in the third eye that I may see,
Put them in my voice that I may sing.
Put them in my heart that I may feel.
Put them in my feet that I may understand.
Make my body healthy, keep my body well.

Several Color quotes that I enjoy and will share.

"Mere color, unspoiled by meaning, and unallied with definite form, can speak to the soul in a thousand different ways." — Oscar Wilde

"Why do two colors, put one next to the other, sing? Can one really explain this? no. Just as one can never learn how to paint." — Pablo Picasso

"Let me, O let me bathe my soul in colors; let me swallow the sunset and drink the rainbow." — Kahlil Gibran

"Color directly influences the soul. Color is the keyboard, the eyes are the hammers, the soul is the piano with many strings. The artist is the hand that plays, touching one key or another purposively, to cause vibrations in the soul." — Wassily Kandinsky, Concerning the Spiritual in Art

"Creation is the vocal cords of God speaking each day through the colors of the sunrise, the vastness of the night sky, the teeming of life in the ocean, the majesty of the mountains." — Eric Samuel Timm, Static Jedi: The Art of Hearing God Through the Noise

CHAPTER EIGHTEEN
THE SENSES

After my first Near Death Experience, I had lots of questions I wanted answered, and the most important one was, why did I come back, and what am I supposed to do now. My guide Om asks the question of the masters, and they said, "She was sent back to be a teacher of the knowing that has no language. The seeing that has no eyes and the hearing that hears the sounds of Cosmic Geometry.

SENSES

Did you ever taste a rainbow,
with bands in every hue?
Or listened to a red sunset,
blazing on clouds of blue?
Have you ever seen the fragrance
that radiates from a rose.
Or have you smelled the dewdrop,
in its crystal-puddled pose?
Have you ever touched a feeling
that swells inside of you?
Well, I have, and
I'll bet you have too.

Senses are the ability of the body to perceive an exterior stimulus and translate it into an understandable form of information that your brain can input and your mind can output. The reason your senses are so important is that they feed information to you as an experience. Once you experience something you know it is a fact. If you heard something, no one could convince you otherwise. If you saw a spaceship, it was photographed in your memory, and no one is going to convince you it was a balloon. If you felt a spirit touch you, that is proof positive that ghosts exist, and if you smell a skunk, you are sure it was not just the trash you forgot to dump. Once you experience something, you own it. This is the importance of conscious observation of your sensory input when singing your songs. And involving as many senses as possible in your songs helps transmit that information to the needed areas.

We normally consider that we have five senses: sight, smell, hearing, taste, and touch. How about feeling, awareness, intuition, and hundreds of emotional senses like understanding, love, anger, pain, and disappointment? Did you know that your senses extend far beyond the basic five? It is important to know that you have other senses, and the most important sense you have and probably have never considered as a sense is common sense.

Your senses are the most useful tools you have, so don't

just take them for granted. You can see how important it is to understand the simple things about your senses when you realize they are responsible for collecting all the information that addresses your brain.

You can control the exposure to information as well as its use in your body. If you realize that you are always in control, you can use your senses to their best potential.

The most important senses you have, and probably never considered as senses, are common sense, and sense of humor.

In "De Anima" [Of the Soul] Aristotle states that every sense must have a sense organ, so according to him we have five senses. According to John Hopkins University, we have nine senses.

Vision [ophthalmoception]
Hearing [audioception]
Smell [olfacoception]
Taste [gustaoception]
Touch [tactioception]
Balance [equilibrioception]
Temperature [thermoception]
Pain [nociception]
Kinesthetic [proprioception]

Then you can add the psychic senses of clairvoyance, clairaudience, clairsentience, clairscent, clairtangency, and clairgustance. The list could go as long as your physical and emotional sensitivity could be creative.

VISION
Vision is the ability to see and to enable that we have two types of receptors called cones and rods, one for color and one for brightness. It is the ability to focus and detect objects and to detect varying colors, brightness and hues. The Rods are sensitive to light but do not detect color, whereas the cones distinguish colors and shades of color.

HEARING
Hearing is all about sound waves and vibrations, and our ear that has the ability to detect this vibration and translate it into a sound. Hearing is a mechanical sense because of the mechanical motion of the fibers in the inner ear.

SMELL
This sense is closely connected with taste in that it is a chemical reaction on sensing surfaces. There are more receptors for smelling than there are for tasting, so we smell much more than we taste. If you cannot smell it is called anosmia.

TASTE
We say we can taste which means we are aware of five different tastes; sweet, sour, salty, bitter, and umami, which is the ability to taste glutamates, especially monosodium glutamate, and nucleotides. We can taste

certain minerals and often recognize a poison substance. The inability to taste is called ageusia.

TOUCH
This is to reach out and touch that is distinct in degrees of touch, pressure, pain, itch, sensors, and temperature. This involves pressure receptors that recognize soft, firm, brushing, squeezing and many more. One can detect pain, hurt, itch, numb, prickling and tingling to list a few more.

BALANCE: EQUILIBRIOCEPTION
This is the sense that lets you balance yourself and also perceive gravity. It is called the labyrinthine system and is part of the inner ear. It senses the motion of the fluid in three canals of the inner ear and keeps you upright as you move from place to place.

TEMPERATURE: THERMOCEPTION
This is the ability to sense hot and cold not only outside the body but also the internal body parts.

PAIN: NOCICEPTION
It was often thought that pain was the overload on the touch sense, but that was found to be untrue. There are three types of pain receptors: somatic is for bones and joints, cutaneous for skin, and visceral for the organs.

KINESTHETIC: PROPRIOCEPTION

This is a sense that most of us know, but know nothing about. The sense that you know where your body parts are, for example, shut your eyes and with your first finger on your right hand touch the tip of your nose. With your eyes still closed hold your arms straight in front of you, point the first finger on each hand toward each other and make the fingers touch.

CLAIRVOYANCE

A Clairvoyant has the ability to see visual objects on other planes of existence. It is usually in the form of shapes, colors, images, pictures or items. It can be in motion or still shot and can often tell a story of history or coming events. It comes from the third eye and can be seen with the physical eyes open or closed. This intensity is gauged by your intuitive powers.

CLAIRAUDIENCE

This is the ability to hear outside the normal sound range, often hearing with your mind not your ears. Often it is an ability of musicians, dancers, composers, writers, etc. It is the ability to hear using a Psychic sense. It is called the paranormal way to hear sounds, voices, and words. There are two forms; you can hear thoughts within your head utilizing your inner ear, or you can hear the sound outside yourself in a conventional way. Either way it is information passing from one person to another without physical contact.

CLAIRSENTIENCE

This is related to feeling and the sense of touch with the ability to perceive energy from the physical sense of touch. One can feel the presence of entities as well as auras and other vibrations. When you sense something will happen and it does, good or bad, that is the sense of clairsentience. These people can easily focus on a person's feeling and pick up on things in the future.

CLAIRSCENT

It means you have a physic sniffer with the ability to smell odors that might have been there long ago, or are coming from another existence. One can detect ethereal odors.

CLAIRTANGENCY

This is the physic sense of touch and is used in psychometry. This is when you hold an object and read the history of the object by its memory vibes.

CLAIRGUSTANCE

This is the ability to perceive taste with your psychic sense. This is the ability to know the existence of something on the ethereal realms by tasting.

Not included in the above list is common sense and sense of humor. The sense of common things and our ability to think we are funny.

COMMON SENSE

It is using sound and practical judgment, down to earth, a matter of fact. It is the ability to make decisions without special training, and live in a safe way, a form of animal intelligence. It is also good sense, shrewdness, insight, capability, native wit, levelheadedness, wisdom, practicality, sensibleness, and resourcefulness.

Aristotle was the first person to record information on common sense. He described it as the ability of all animals, including humans, to process sensory perceptions, imagination and memory to make reflex judgments. He added that humans have the addition of reasoning and thinking that advance them above just common sense. He theorized that the animal mind converted raw sense perceptions into five specialized senses, and common sense is their ability to file information properly without crossing item with the response. You taste what you eat, instead of hearing that something is sweet. Rene Descartes states in his, "Discourse on Method," that everyone has a similar amount of common sense, but they rarely use it properly.

SENSE OF HUMOR

If you have a sense of humor, you can laugh at yourself while at the same time taking yourself seriously. You can create humor and make jokes. You can change places with your audience to check their responses to you. You can laugh at others and with others. You can know and exercise discretion when fooling around in public. You can appreciate others jokes without your ego interfering. If you have a good sense of humor, you can honorably accept constructive criticism.

Your Senses are extremely important to your survival. They feed your body vital information, nourish your organs with life-giving sustenance and introduce you to new challenges in life. Senses are one of the things that science cannot perfect when they attempt to produce artificial intelligence.

In the 70's a group of influential researchers organized a summer project of introducing artificial intelligence to their computer. Their accumulative intelligence fostered by their ego compelled them to believe they could master this project in a few months. 45 years later however they are still stumbling over barricades of self-imposed limitations. Although there has been a great advancement in the technology of artificial intelligence it is accomplished only by the incorporation and magnification of the human senses.

The human body was equipped with a hard drive with a limitless source of gigabytes these challenges and wins over the fastest computers we are capable of producing. Our software is copyrighted by nature and hides its secrets from the scrutiny of probing test tubes, Petri dishes, and laboratory testing equipment. Our scientific world has no problem identifying body parts, dissecting their complicated structures and tracking their electrons to the brain. However, the part of the brain we call the mind is totally unknown to them because it has no physical form, and they cannot dissect it. It is the part of the brain that we are dealing with in this theory of mind control.

In our study of hypnosis, self-hypnosis, meditation and visualization it is important to understand that your brain is an amazing network of neutrons that give the brain information by processing everything your senses perceive. The first challenge for any sensory system is to translate the physical and chemical energy of its exposed information into potential activities, known as transduction. Each of our senses utilizes transduction in its fashion, but each has the same purpose, which is transporting information from our environment to our brain.

CONCLUSIONS

In conclusion: I hope my story has been helpful to you, and that it has inspired you to share your story; that it might be helpful to someone else. Always remember, all it takes is to have faith in yourself that equals the size of a mustard seed, and you can heal yourself.

Luke 13:19 KJV

It is like a grain of mustard seed, which a man took, and cast into his garden: and it grew, and waxed a great tree; and the fowls of the air lodged in the branches of it.

Update and Validation.

This book was initially published in 2014 titled Singing in the Brain. Giving you instructions on how to stay healthy or at least stay alive. That was 11 years ago, so something in the book must work, as I was 75 then and 86 now. So, I will update you and validate my ups and downs and the reason I am still alive, although death keeps knocking on my door. The truth is you don't know what you have until you lose it. Life must be tested for you to really appreciate it and I have been tested many times. I enjoy waking up every morning and looking forward to my 86 birthday in a couple of weeks.

When I died for the first time in 1985, I never dreamed that I would see this age. Or that I would be capable of my mental and physical activities.

Let's digress to 11 years ago and see what the Grim Reaper had for me in his bag of tricks. He pretty much left me alone until 2017, when a colonoscopy went bad and turned into diverticulitis that hospitalized me twice and sent me to oncology for a PET scan that showed that nasty 'C' word. I was off to MD Anderson in Houston Tx where they Biopsied my liver and named the 'C' Non-Hodgin large cell Lymphoma. For the next six months, they treated me for that Problem while acknowledging that the sarcoma they removed in my right thigh in Jan 1992 had returned. On Christmas Eve 2018, I finished 6 months of chemo, and the PET scan said ALL GONE. Today, in 2025, 6 years later, it is still gone, although the sarcoma came home with me, and I still drag it around. The chemo was not pleasant to my heart and put me in perpetual A-fib until 6 months ago.

This past year, I had my sixth heart device installed; after five pacemakers, I now have a defibration. Two months after I received my new device, I found myself referencing a dog fight in my living room, and the defibrillator shocked me and a month later, I got COVID, and it shocked me again. The second jolt put my heart into sinus mode, where it has stayed for the past six months, and I am doing GREAT.

This is the cave where Mother Earth breathes her blessings on me. If you are silent and listen closely you can hear her whisper to you. NO, she does not speak English, she speaks Cosmos. In 2025 she is crying for the planet and all its INNOCENT LIFE

Jeri Lee C.Ht.

Kathy died in 1991. Twenty years later I had a Ceremony of LIFE at the entrance to the cave of Mother Earth's Mouth on the land we shared. To Acknowledge her Absence and Our Love. I threw her ashes into the air; they formed a large bird that came back to me.

Jeri Lee C.Ht.

Jeri R. Lee C.Ht.

ABOUT THE AUTHOR

Jeri R. Lee was born May 1, 1939. Being a Beltane Child she went in search of her magical powers. She was that childish leprechaun that hypnotized her father's chickens and talked to the farm animals, while knowing at a young age she was searching for the pot of gold from her inner rainbow.

In the 60's her career went from layout artist to technical illustrator. In the 70's she started creating jewelry along with her growing interest in the Tarot, Palmistry, Astrology, Ancient history and Mythology. These new interests inspired a unique style of jewelry with occult influences that was fitting for the 'new age'.

In the 80's and 90's, her Art creations took her from Art shows to Renaissance Fairs and now to the Internet. She specializes in symbols, which are the cosmic geometric patterns of consciousness.

Form 92 to 2010 she raised dogs and showed in AKC competition. She is credited with about 97 AKC Champion Chinese Cresteds.

Now at age 76 her interest has turned to healing through hypnosis. She studied under the late Dolores Cannon and at age 75 she flew to CA to be an active part of her graduating class of 2014 at Hypnosis Motivation Institute, receiving a diploma for a career she started as a child.

**My symbols
for**

Universal Peace

I spent many years in the research and study of cultural anthropology relating to the origin of man and his beliefs. The one basic truth that I found is that both man and his traditions go back to one origin, and that All Humans go back to a single source that was genetically modified and influenced by space travelers. Also that Astronomy is the elementary science, .and Astrology is its theology it is the original religion. All religions are theologies having the same thread of truth weaving itself through each of them. Whether they are considered modern or ancient their Gods are the Hero of their evolution and their symbols are their signature. Based on that I took the symbols of the worlds ancient religions and assembled them into the standard shape of the cross. I named it the **"All is One Cross"** and labeled it my concept of Universal Peace

More Book by
Jeri Lee

Jeri Lee C.Ht.

You Might enjoy one of my many coloring books, Most of which are designed with Adults in mind.

My Coloring books are 8.5 x 11 with 50 to 100 pages to color. They are focused on Save the Planet and pages can be purchases on Amazon.com

www.ingramcontent.com/pod-product-compliance
Lightning Source LLC
Chambersburg PA
CBHW031239290426
44109CB00012B/358